Communication at Work

Communication at Work

Florence Little, BA

Lecturer in Communication Studies
St John's College of Further Education, Manchester

HODDER AND STOUGHTON
LONDON SYDNEY AUCKLAND TORONTO

British Library Cataloguing in Publication Data

Little, Florence

Communication at work.
1. Communication.
2. Communication in management.
I. Title
001.5'02'4658 P90

ISBN 0 340 25264 2

Printed and bound in Great Britain for
Hodder and Stoughton Educational,
a division of Hodder and Stoughton Ltd,
Mill Road, Dunton Green, Sevenoaks, Kent,
by Richard Clay (The Chaucer Press) Ltd,
Bungay, Suffolk.

Phototypesetting by Swiftpages Limited, Liverpool.

Contents

Introduction

This book is about communication. It is about the ways we transmit our thoughts and feelings to other people, either by speaking or by writing, and receive other people's thoughts and feelings, either by listening or by reading. We all, whatever we may do for a living, get more out of life if we can communicate well and with ease, but in some occupations it is impossible to function efficiently unless we can do so. This is particularly the case if we work with people, in the service of the public as employees of central or local government, or in business. When we listen to someone talking, we must be able to pick out the essential points of what is being said and retain them in our memory. This is very important, for instance, when we are being given instructions of any kind.

Good listening eliminates not only misunderstanding, but also the need for time-wasting repetition. We must train ourselves to be able to write while we are listening: not to scribble away furiously, trying to put down every word that is being said and getting hopelessly left behind, but to select intelligently the main points and note them as concisely as possible, so that we can use them later as a framework for an expanded version, or report, of what we heard.

Similarly, when we read something, we need to be able to extract the main points and remember them, to make notes of these points, and to understand our notes when we come back to them.

In public life it is important to know how to express what we have to say as clearly and simply as possible, both in speech and in writing, so that all sections of the community can understand us, regardless of the differences in their backgrounds and education. This requires a thorough understanding of what words mean and how they are used. We must be able to put words together correctly into sentences, divide up what we are saying into paragraphs, invent headings and sub-headings to help people find their way through the material. We must also master the art of presenting what we have to say as attractively as possible, both by choosing our words carefully, and by setting out our written communications to display them to maximum effect.

All these aspects of listening and speaking, reading and writing, are dealt with in this book. Each chapter is self-contained, but students who feel that they need to work through from the beginning to the end will find that the progression is carefully graded from basic word skills in Section 1, through the techniques of letter writing, précis, comprehension and composition in Sections 2, 3 and 4, to less familiar skills of oral communication, Report Writing, Minutes and other forms of communication in the last four sections. A careful study of this book and the exercises it contains should bring the student up to the level of proficiency required to cope with the Business Education Council's National Level course.

1

Fundamentals of Communication

Words, their meaning and use

Expanding your vocabulary

Have you ever thought of the large number of words you never use, although you know the meaning of them?

So often, we are satisfied to use a word which means *approximately* what we want to say, without stopping to consider whether we could have selected one closer to our *exact* meaning.

Look at the following sentences, and see how many times the writer has used the word 'nice':

> On a nice day in August, when the weather was nice and warm, Stephen and his sister Susan went for a nice bicycle ride in the country. They stopped at midday for a nice meal and a nice rest, and then made their way home through the lanes to arrive nice and tired in time for a nice big tea.

Now let's see what can be done when the writer takes a little more trouble to examine his vocabulary and select words from it which convey a more precise meaning:

> On a fine day in August, when the weather was bright and warm, Stephen and his sister Susan went for an enjoyable bicycle ride in the country. They stopped at midday for a welcome meal and a refreshing rest, and then made their way home through the lanes to arrive pleasantly tired in time for a delicious big tea.

It still isn't great literature, but it is undoubtedly an improvement on the earlier version.

See if you can improve the following passage by substituting a more satisfactory word or phrase every time the writer has used 'got':

> When I got up this morning, I got out of bed and got a shock when I realised what time it was. I realised I had got to hurry up if I wasn't to be late for work. I got a quick wash, got my clothes on, got downstairs, and realised I hadn't got time for any breakfast. So I got an apple from the sideboard and got out of the house as fast as I

could. I just got the bus at the corner of the street, and when I got to work I nearly collapsed with exhaustion and relief.

If you are working in class, compare your version with those of the other members of the class, and count up the total number of new words you have introduced into the passage.

Did you notice that the writer has used 'realised' three times? Can you think of any other words to substitute for it?

So often when we are speaking we fall into the habit of using just a few words over and over again, when we have so many more at our disposal.

Using words correctly

Of course, we do have to be careful when we start to expand our vocabulary to make sure that we are using the less familiar words correctly.

Exercise 1.1. Here is a list of words which are frequently mis-used. Consult your dictionary to discover the true meanings, and then write a sentence for each word, using it correctly and bringing out this real meaning as clearly as you can:

aggravate	chronic	disinterested	emulate	fantastic
incredulous	livid	notorious	pathetic	transpire

Exercise 1.2. Complete each of the following sentences by inserting in the blank space the most appropriate of the words in brackets:

(*a*) Most companies are prepared to offer a . . . . discount on large orders. (substantive, subversive, substantial)
(*b*) In addition, regular . . . . may enjoy special credit facilities. (buyers, customers, clients)
(*c*) However, abuse of these facilities may result in their . . . . (withdrawal, abeyance, stoppage)
(*d*) This is sound . . . . in view of the competitive nature of business. (practice, practise)
(*e*) After all, the supplier himself has to meet the costs of raw materials and . . . . his staff. (remunerate, pay, reimburse)
(*f*) Therefore it is wise not to attempt to . . . . the privilege of extended credit. (abuse, overdo, exercise)

Exercise 1.3. Write a sentence for each of the words in Exercise 1.2 which you did not use in the sentences there, bringing out the meaning as clearly and precisely as possible.

Spelling

Another use for your dictionary is in checking the spelling of a word when you are unsure. Because there are so many inconsistencies in English spelling, it is difficult to establish a set of rules, and many words can be learned only by looking them up in the dictionary and familiarising yourself with the way they are spelt.

Exercise 1.4. The following passage contains a number of common words which are frequently misspelt. Look up the correct spellings and correct the passage:

> On the question of new gas fires in the sheltered acomodation, the superintendant said a desision had been deffered untill the abscent members of the comittee were availible for a discusion. He did not wish any embarassment to be caused to those offisers who had to instal the new apliances in the bungallows, but sincereley beleived that the tenents would feel less agreived at haveing to wait for their new equippment than by haveing it instaled and then removed again. Nobody benefitted from regretable haste. At this point there was an interuption from the ecentric Mr Jones, who surgested that the old people should borrow extra woolens from their nieghbours.

'Commercialese'

Language is often abused by people in public life particularly. 'Jargon' employs many words where a few would do, and invents expressions to say things which can be said just as easily in simple language that everyone understands. Many people blame the social sciences for the spread of jargon, but in fairness to sociologists and psychologists it must be admitted that very often they are dealing with new concepts, or combinations of ideas, and so they need new words to express them. There is no such excuse for 'commercialese', though. This is the name given to the unnecessarily complicated and obscure language often used in business letters.

Exercise 1.5. Here is an example of a letter written in 'commercialese'. Re-write it without all the unnecessarily complicated expressions and saying what you have to say as clearly and simply as possible:

Frazer & Brown Ltd,
Richmond Road,
Oldbury.
OB1 8DF

18th February, 1980.

Messrs U.N. Atherne,
Paradise Works,
BRADSTONE.
BR2 6RZ

Dear Sir,

We beg to acknowledge receipt of your esteemed communication dated 15th inst.

Re your valued enquiry re our "Olive Branch" greenhouse, we are able to quote you a price of £87.00 for the standard model, with a figure of £101.86 applying if your enquiry relates to the de-luxe version.

We are forwarding to you under separate cover our catalogue of goods and prices, and shall have pleasure in arranging for delivery to be expedited immediately upon receipt of your valued instructions.

Assuring you of our prompt and courteous attention at all times,

We remain,

Yours faithfully,

For Frazer & Brown Ltd
Managing Director

If you have done this exercise correctly, your version of the letter should be considerably shorter than the original. When you consider how many letters are sent out from most offices in a day, a week, or a year, you will realise what enormous savings in time, labour and materials—which all cost money—can be made by avoiding superfluous words.

Giving and following instructions

When someone asks you how to get to a certain place, can you tell him or her without using your arms to point directions? Do you automatically start to make sweeping gestures in mid-air when you say 'left' or 'right'?

See if you can manage without such non-verbal aids. Ask another member of the class (or someone else, if you are working at home) to sit back-to-back with you. You should each have a piece of lined paper and a pen or pencil. Draw a geometrical design on your paper, and as you do so, instruct your partner as clearly as possible what to do in order to copy your actions. You may use statistics, such as 'now continue this line horizontally to the left for about six centimetres', or you may use relations, such as 'under this circle, draw a triangle', or any other *verbal* method you can find to convey your meaning as exactly as possible. After a few minutes, stop and compare the two versions of the drawing. If they are not exactly alike, try again, with the 'following' partner leading this time.

If after the second try you are still producing differing results, you might like to try again with a variation this time; allow the 'follower' to ask questions in order to clarify the instructions given by the 'leader'.

Has this activity helped to show you how much we tend to rely on non-verbal means, and on questioning, when we are giving and following instructions? There is nothing wrong in resorting to such aids, of course, but the difficulty is that when we give *written* instructions, we cannot use our arms, legs, or heads to indicate what to do or which way to go. Nor can our 'follower' always contact us to ask for clarification.

Now draw a house on a piece of paper, and write down instructions for drawing an identical house. Pass your instructions, but not the drawing, to someone else, and let him or her try to follow them.

If the houses are not identical, where did you go wrong? Was it in not specifying the size or position of the windows? Did you forget to say in which direction the wind was blowing the smoke from the chimney? Or did you use a word which was unfamiliar to your 'follower' so that he or she had to guess at its meaning?

Chronological order

Chronos is the Greek word for 'time', and 'chronological order' is the order in which things happen in time. If we are to succeed in instructing someone how to do something, we will need to think about the order in which the different stages come.

Exercise 1.6. Write an account of how to do one of the following, numbering the different stages:

(*a*) Make a cup of coffee
(*b*) Repair a puncture in a bicycle tyre
(*c*) Make up your face
(*d*) Arrive outside the local main-line rail station, starting from where you are now

Pass your instructions to someone else, and ask if they are clear and easy to follow, or if perhaps you have taken something so much for granted that you have forgotten to mention it.

Describing people

If someone were to come to you and ask how he or she could recognise one of your friends or colleagues, could you give a clear and accurate description of the person as a help in finding him or her?

Look at the two descriptions of Mrs Healey that follow, and decide which you think would be more useful if you were trying to locate her:

A. Oh yes, Mrs Healey—she's a horrible little fat bad-tempered woman with frizzy hair and she's always shouting at people.
B. Mrs Healey is about five feet tall and measures approximately forty inches round the hips. She has short mid-brown hair and a louder-than-average voice and tends to move quickly and rather irritably.

Why is one of these descriptions much better than the other? Have you ever considered that Mrs Healey is only thought 'little' by people who are taller than she is, or 'fat' by those who are thinner? And although her hair may be 'frizzy' to you if yours is long and straight, it may be merely 'wavy' to someone who has an 'Afro' hairstyle. Description A is too *subjective*: it depends for its validity on the personal views of the speaker, or writer. On the other hand, description B tries to be *objective*: it attempts to present Mrs Healey in terms of statistics, and by comparing her voice with others. The obvious advantage of this kind of description is that it uses words and ideas which are readily understood by almost everyone.

Exercise 1.7. Write three paragraphs of about ten lines each, describing as objectively as possible:

(*a*) A well known politician
(*b*) A person from the world of sport or entertainment
(*c*) A member of your class

Test your descriptions by reading them out or giving them to someone else to read. If they are instantly recognised, they are good descriptions.

Describing things

When we describe things—objects—we can adopt a systematic plan. A good way of beginning a description is to state the purpose of the object. For example, a washing machine is for washing clothes, not babies; and whereas we put documents inside a document case, we do not carry our hands around in a handbag. Having stated what the purpose of the object is, we can then move on to an objective description of its properties, just as we listed Mrs Healey's properties. An object has material existence, it is made of something: wood, plastic, leather and metal, glass, or whatever. It also has dimensions—not large and small, but actual measurements. Objects are shaped, they are cubes or spheres or shaped like other familiar objects with which it may be useful to compare them. Colour comes into this, too. Then, with more complicated pieces of equipment there can follow an explanation of how this object fulfils the purpose for which it is intended: does it work by electricity or is it mechanically operated?

The main points to bear in mind when describing anything at all are:

(*a*) *Give as much information as possible which will distinguish your object from other, similar, things.* For example, 'a daisy is a flower' or 'a chair is for sitting on' are not good descriptions, because lots of other kinds of flowers exist, and we can sit on other things besides chairs. Try to write a more exhaustive description of each of these two things, so that someone who had never seen either of them would be able to recognize them in future.

(*b*) *Make sure you have not included in your description any information which limits it and excludes some objects of the kind you are describing.* For example, 'A chair is a wooden object intended for sitting on' is a bad description, because there are metal chairs, chairs of mixed composition, and even inflatable rubber and plastic chairs.

Exercise 1.8. Write brief definitions of the following objects, bearing in mind all the points made above:

a suitcase	an evening bag	a tool box
a weekend case	a toilet bag	a telephone box

Exercise 1.9. Here are a few modern inventions. Choose one of them, and write a description explaining what the invention is, for someone who has been asleep since 1895:

a cassette recorder	heated rollers	a word processor
a blender-grinder	a domestic freezer	a photo-copying machine

Exercise 1.10. Write a full description of the area in which you live, to give as much information as possible to someone thinking of coming to live there. Your description should be purely objective.

Putting words together

It is easy to put words together in any old order, but if we want to communicate efficiently, we have to find ways of putting them together which best convey our meaning.

Sentences

The best definition of a sentence that I know is 'a group of words that makes complete sense'. 'Under the greenwood tree' makes some sort of sense, since we all know what is meant by 'under' and we can imagine 'the greenwood tree' without too much difficulty. But the sense is not complete, because we do not know what happened under the greenwood tree. 'George sat down under the greenwood tree' is complete, because we know both what happened and to whom it happened.

Look at these two groups of words:

Birds fly.
Brown birds

One is a sentence, and one is not. 'Birds fly' can have a full stop after it, because it makes complete sense, but 'Brown birds' does not. Perhaps you will immediately say 'Birds fly' contains a *verb,* whereas there is no verb in 'Brown birds'. However, some people have difficulty in understanding or remembering what a verb is. Quite simply, a verb is a *doing* word or, occasionally, a *being* word. In every sentence, there must be a verb, to indicate what is going on, what the sentence is about. And of course, we also want to know who or what is performing the action, *doing*, or being.

Find the verbs in the following sentences:

The sun sank slowly in the west.
The cat sat on the mat.
Down the road came Billy the Kid.
What time will the train get in?

Now ask yourself in each case which word, or group of words, is responsible for the action indicated by the verb.

What sank?
What sat?
Who came?
What will get in?

These words, which are responsible for the action, are called *subjects.*

If you understand what a verb is, and what is meant by a subject, and if you remember that every sentence has to have both a verb and a subject, you will never write an incomplete sentence again.

To make sure that you have grasped the idea, re-write the following incomplete groups of words into sentences, making sure that each has a verb and a subject:

(*a*) Referring to your letter of 27 May
(*b*) Floating through the air
(*c*) A nasty smell on the landing
(*d*) Three blind mice
(*e*) Over the mountains and far away

Questions

A question is a special kind of sentence. We saw in 'What time will the train get in?' that questions need verbs and subjects if they are to make complete sense. But whereas an ordinary sentence *gives* information, a question seeks it.

Write the questions which are answered by each of the following sentences:

(*a*) The young lady's name is Sandra Brown.
(*b*) The sun sank.
(*c*) I have just been to the Post Office.
(*d*) We will get home at seven o'clock.
(*e*) George had a pork chop for his tea.

Did you remember to put a question mark at the end each time?

Whenever a group of words seeks information, a question mark is necessary. Thus 'What time is it?' requires one, as does 'Is it seven o'clock yet?' and even 'It's never seven o'clock already?'

However, when we are *reporting* the fact that someone asked for information *in the past,* we do not need a question mark. An example of this is 'I asked him the time', or 'I asked him what time it was'. These are statements *about* questions, not questions themselves. A very simple rule to remember about this is that we need a question mark after *the actual words used* by the questioner (direct speech) but not otherwise (reported speech).

Which of the following groups of words require question marks, and which do not?

(*a*) I asked the time of the next train
(*b*) When are we going to Grandmother's
(*c*) Are you coming to the dance on Saturday
(*d*) He wanted to know what I had in my pocket
(*e*) Shall we go home now
(*f*) You're not hungry again already

Exclamations

Another kind of sentence is the exclamation, followed by an exclamation mark (!). Sometimes, when we are quoting direct speech, using the actual words which someone uttered, we need to indicate that the tone of voice in which the words were spoken was an excited one. An instance of this is 'Push off!'. Because exclamation marks have a very specific purpose, we should avoid using them unnecessarily, so that they retain their full effectiveness for when we really need them.

Implied subjects

Taking the little group of words 'Push off!' you may have been wondering 'Where is the subject here?' The answer is that it is *implied.* The subject is *you,* the person who is being addressed, and because this person knows that he or she is being addressed, there is no need to say 'You push off.' Ideally, of course, one hopes not to have to resort to this kind of language at all.

However, there are other occasions when we imply the subject 'you' rather than state it directly. In giving instructions of how to get somewhere, for instance, we do not always say 'You must turn left at the first traffic lights'. 'Turn left at the first traffic lights' will do just as well, and the subject is implied.

Quotation marks

You will have noticed that throughout the preceding paragraphs, wherever words or phrases have been *quoted,* they have been enclosed in inverted commas, or quotation marks. This is a very useful device of punctuation. Quotation marks are used to indicate the actual words which a speaker uttered, and also when quoting *verbatim* (word for word) from a document, a book, or any previously prepared material.

It is useful to introduce quotations by putting a colon (:) at the end of the preamble, thus:

> In your letter of 17th March, you stated:
>
> 'The newspaper you have requested is unfortunately not available in this country.'

When quoting words spoken in conversation, it is customary to begin a fresh paragraph every time there is a change of speaker.

You will find a fuller explanation of verbs and other parts of speech, and a discussion of the uses of the different punctuation marks, in the Appendix at the end of this book.

Exercise 1.11. Write *Sentences* to bring out clearly the meanings of the following words:

subjective	verbatim	colloquial	jargon	significance
prospective	appraisal	capacity	concisely	digression
relatively	implications	specific	relevant	diplomatic

Exercise 1.12. Punctuate the following passage, bearing in mind what a sentence needs to be complete:

> whether you work in a private business or in local government or the civil service whether you work in a bank or a building society no doubt you have ambitions perhaps these ambitions have been with

you since your schooldays and you now feel that you are on the way to achieving them or perhaps you have only formed your ambitions since starting work however this may be you will help yourself towards your goal of a successful career by obtaining as much knowledge and as many qualifications as you can do you sometimes regret that you wasted so much time at school and wish that you could have a second chance well you can there are classes available at your local college for just this purpose to enable you to catch up on what you missed whether it was through your own negligence or for some other reason most colleges have evening classes in the kinds of subjects which will help you to progress in your business career from shorthand and typing and bookkeeping to languages so essential in the days of the common market in addition many employers are willing to allow young employees to attend college during business hours through the system known as day release which confers all the benefits of an apprenticeship on those who have the good sense to take advantage of it so why not find out about the courses that are available in your area when you find out how easy and enjoyable it is to climb the ladder of success youll be glad you did

Exercise 1.13. Turn the following into reported speech, omitting all quotation marks and using the past tense:

'I'm dreadfully sorry, Mr Smith, but I thought I'd better let you know right away that the components I promised you for Thursday won't be ready now until Friday morning at the earliest.'

'But Mr Young! You told me quite definitely I could have them on Thursday. I said Wednesday night at first, then left it till Thursday, and now you say I can't have them till Friday!'

'Yes, and I am sorry, but unfortunately we had a power failure in the factory yesterday afternoon and the men who were going to do overtime went home. The power's on again now, but we're several hours behind schedule.'

'That's all very well, Young, but what am I going to tell my customer? I've promised him these parts for Thursday morning at the latest so that he can fly them out to his Company abroad, and now this!'

'Well, as I said, Mr Smith, I'm sorry, but I don't really see that there's anything more I can do about it . . .'

'Well, I'll tell you one thing, Young, it's the last time you'll get a chance to mess up an order of mine.'

Exercise 1.14. Punctuate the following, setting it out correctly:

14 heyridge drive north fleet west suffolk 17 may 1980 the manager braden and co ltd brierly buildings oxford road burnden bn2 7sx dear sir i am writing to ask if you have any vacancies in your company for management trainees i left school two years ago with three passes at o level in english language maths and geography and cse grade one in french and art since then i have been employed by rogers wallpapers of colchester as a management trainee and have been attending a business studies course part time but now my family is moving to burnden and i am forced to seek employment in that area my departmental manager mr brian

redmond suggested that i should approach you and said that he would give me a reference i would be able to attend for an interview at any time if required yours faithfully derek wilson

Exercise 1.15. Here is a reported extract from a speech. Re-write it in the words you think the speaker actually used:

The Director explained the train of events which had led to the necessity for the redundancies. When he had bought the business five years previously it had been a very small concern employing only a very few people. From the beginning he had had the intention of building it up and making it into a prosperous enterprise. He had wanted this not only for himself, but for all his employees as well. Since they were the people who made the prosperity, it was only right that they should share in it. Therefore he had looked around for ways of increasing business and about two years previously he had entered into partnership with Mr Johnson. Then they had purchased Cassidy and Company and taken on all their staff, and things had seemed to be going very well. However, for the past six months the takings had been steadily decreasing and a situation had been reached where the volume of business being turned over was simply not sufficient to meet costs, let alone provide any profit at the end of the day. He said he wondered whether any of his listeners had ever calculated the weekly wages bill for the company, and told them that it exceeded ten thousand pounds. During several recent weeks there had not been enough production in the factory to cover that amount alone. He reminded them that wages were not the only production cost. There were also rent and rates, bills for electricity and gas, and of course the cost of raw materials. In that connection, things had become so bad that one supplier had refused to extend any further credit until his outstanding account was settled. He had, he said, racked his brains to think of an alternative solution, but in spite of all the efforts which Mr Johnson had made to attract new customers, the orders just had not been coming in. Reluctantly he had to admit that Drayton-Cassidy were losing business to other manufacturers because their prices were not sufficiently competitive. And although it was very hard to accept, the reason for the inability to compete was the very large wages bill. He concluded by saying that although he and Mr Johnson were both still willing to listen to any ideas anyone had for solving the problem in another way, he had called that morning's meeting to explain that he would be contacting the Union that day to discuss redundancy procedures. He apologised.

2

Letters and Memoranda

Writing a letter

The letter is the most familiar kind of written communication. There are many different kinds of letters, but they all have certain things in common, and almost everyone receives and writes letters at some time. There are certain conventions about setting out letters, which will be familiar to everyone, but it is worthwhile refreshing our memories at this point.

If we take a simple business letter written by an individual by hand as our first example, we have to remember that:

1. *The address of the sender* should appear at the top of the page, on the right-hand side. The address ought to include the postcode.
2. *The date* should be written *in full* beneath the sender's address, for example: 17 November 1980.
3. Lower down the page, on the left-hand side, we include the *name and address* of the person or organisation to whom the letter is to be sent. All business letters must include this 'inside address'. It is best to try to discover the individual within an organisation to whom the letter should be addressed, as this avoids delays.
4. Beneath the recipient's name and address we leave a small space, and then write the *salutation.* This often takes the form 'Dear Sir,' but if we know the person to whom we are writing we may wish to adopt a more personal tone, and write 'Dear Mr Jenkins,'. Whichever form we adopt, we have to remember to begin each word with a capital letter and to put a comma at the end of the salutation.
5. Next comes the *body of the letter,* which is the real communication task, where we either impart or ask for information.
6. The letter ends with a *complimentary close.* The rule for this is that if we have begun with the salutation 'Dear Sir,' we must now write 'Yours faithfully,' but 'Dear Mr Jenkins,' at the beginning requires 'Yours sincerely,' at the end. These are the only two alternatives permissible in a business letter, and the punctuation must be strictly adhered to: a capital letter for 'Yours' and a small initial letter for 'faithfully' or 'sincerely', with a comma at the end.

7. The *signature* follows the complimentary close. A person's signature consists of either a first name and a surname, or initials and a surname. If a lady wishes to indicate her marital status, it has been customary in the past for her to put 'Miss' or 'Mrs' in brackets either before or after her name, but with the modern use of 'Ms' to address all ladies, this would appear to have become unnecessary. A signature ought to be readable, but in case it is not, it is permissible to print the name underneath.

Exercise 2.1. Write a letter replying to each of the following advertisements:

(*a*) Manager required, male or female, to run our branch of Montano Delicatessen at 76 Warburton Road, Reddington, Burchester B20 0HN.
(*b*) Killingdon Corporation invites applications from school-leavers for appointment as trainee officers of the Council. Apply in writing to the Staff Officer, Town Hall, Killingdon K12 7FX, quoting reference JD270.
(*c*) Trainee representatives required (male or female) for exciting new business venture. Write with details to B. S. Redford, Box 107, Motley Evening News, Motley M60 3BB.

You should have found no difficulty in setting out your letters correctly, but what about the actual content of your communications? Did you think carefully about what kind of information you ought to give about yourself when applying for a position? The employer would wish to know, as well as your name, address, age and nationality, what kind of qualifications you have to fit you for the post. Where did you go to school? What examinations have you passed, and at what level? Are you awaiting the results of any examinations? In the case of letter (*a*), have you done this kind of work before? How many employers have you had, and for how long did you remain with each one? How much did they pay you? Why did you leave? Both (*b*) and (*c*) are rather vague about the kind of employment that is being offered, and you would be well advised to request more details. Another question the employer will want answered is when you will be available to start working for him. And did you remember to give the names and addresses of people who would provide references or testimonials for you?

Curriculum vitae

If you feel that a letter covering all the details of your qualifications and experience is going to be unwieldy, an acceptable method of applying for a post is to write a short letter stating where you saw the post advertised, and enclose the details about yourself on a separate sheet. Such a data sheet is called a *curriculum vitae* (life history), and should be set out as follows:

NAME:	JENKINS, Peter Brian
ADDRESS:	16 Manor Avenue, Sale, Cheshire M33 5NU
DATE OF BIRTH:	16th January, 1960.
NATIONALITY:	British

EDUCATION

1971 - 7	Sale High School, Yew Tree Lane, Sale, Cheshire M33 6XW
1977 - 8 (part time)	North Trafford College of Further Education, Chester Road, Altrincham, Cheshire WA10 6PB

QUALIFICATIONS

GCE 'O' Level in English Language, English Literature, Geography, History and Scripture.
ULCI Certificate in Office Studies.

EXPERIENCE

1977 - 9	Clerical Assistant, HM Customs & Excise, Portcullis House, Seymour Grove, Manchester M60 7ZT
1979 - 80	Trainee Manager, Printshop Ltd, 3 Queensway, Sale, Cheshire M33 1US

REFERENCES MAY BE OBTAINED FROM

1. Mr J. Lloyd, HM Customs & Excise, Portcullis House, Seymour Grove, Manchester M60 7ZT
2. Mr B. Gardiner, Printshop Ltd, 3 Queensway, Sale, Cheshire M33 1US

You may include under 'Experience' details of the actual duties involved in the posts you have held, as well as your reasons for leaving or wishing to change your employment.

Writing on behalf of an organisation

When you write a letter on behalf of your employer, you will be provided with printed paper carrying the name, address and telephone number of the organisation. It would be a good idea for all the members of your class to display examples of the 'letterheads' used in the offices where they or their friends work, as these can differ quite widely. However, all letterheads will show the name and address, and for examination purposes you may be expected to produce a 'home-made' letterhead which looks convincing in terms of lay-out. This is not as pointless as it may seem, since there may be many occasions when it would be useful for you to be able to design your own: for example, if you were to be secretary of a voluntary organisation, social club, or other such group.

The Reference

Firms, local authorities, government departments and other organisations always assign *references* to correspondence, and these usually appear near the top left-hand corner of the page. This is to ensure ease of delivery to the appropriate individual or section, and is a help in filing. When a letter is received bearing a reference, this should be quoted on the reply, and many letterheads carry the words 'Your reference' and 'Our reference', with a space to be filled in by the writer.

Such a reference often consists of the initials of the person dictating the letter, those of the secretary or typist, and a reference to the file in which the correspondence and other papers are kept.

The Heading

Business and official correspondence often has a heading, just below the salutation and above the body of the letter. Like the reference, this can be very useful in assigning the correspondence as quickly as possible to the person who is best able to deal with it.

The Signature

When you are writing on behalf of a firm or organisation, it is customary to indicate the position which you hold, for example Sales Manager. If your position is a relatively humble one, you may be expected to sign your name over the title of your Head of Department, for example:

D. J. Williams
for CITY TREASURER

Or you may simply sign over the name of the Department or section:

D. J. Williams
CITY TREASURER'S DEPARTMENT

Further variations of these ways of signing occur, including 'Dictated by Mr Williams and signed in his absence'. Each organisation has its own practice, and this is one of the features of 'House Style'.

House Style

Many business firms and organisations like their correspondence to be displayed in a particular way, and this is known as the 'house style'. It involves the spacing, lay-out and punctuation of letters, and must be adhered to by all who write for the organisation in an official capacity, or who type the correspondence.

Exercise 2.2. Write each of the following letters on a suitably designed letterhead:

(*a*) As Secretary of your local Debating Society, write asking a well known person to address the society. (Remember that you will have to offer a choice of dates, and that it is polite to offer to pay any expenses incurred by such a visitor.)

(*b*) Write the letter which you will send out to your members informing them of the arrangements made for the above meeting. (Remember that this letter will be sent to a number of people, so you will have to leave a space for the individual names and addresses to be filled in.)

(*c*) On behalf of a voluntary youth organisation to which you belong, write a letter for publication in the local newspaper, seeking support for a fund-raising event you are organising. (Remember that people donating money to charities like to know the purpose for which it will be used.)

Exercise 2.3.

(*a*) Write a letter to a friend who is about to start a course similar to the one you are following, telling him what to expect and evaluating the usefulness of what you have learned so far.

(*b*) You have recently seen your local disused railway station described as an 'eyesore' in a local paper. This made you angry as you have several friends who believe, as you do, that it could be used in any one of several ways to benefit the community. Write a letter to the newspaper on this subject.

(*c*) Write to the Head of your last school, asking him or her to provide you with a reference to help you in applying for a post in which you are interested.

Finding the right way of saying things

It is important to find the most precise way of expressing our thoughts and feelings in order to communicate them to others. But it is also important that we take into account the thoughts and feelings of the people we are attempting to communicate with, and the nature of the communication itself.

A letter of complaint may require a quite different approach or 'tone' from a letter in reply to a complaint. A letter informing a parent that his or her child cannot go to the school they have chosen will require to be expressed tactfully; helpful suggestions about alternative possibilities should be made. A letter of collection, reminding a customer that payment of an account is overdue, will need to be sufficiently firm to make its point without being so abrupt that it will antagonise him and lose the firm his custom. If we remember that tact and courtesy are *always* suitable, we will be well on the way to avoiding many common errors. This is important when writing business letters, where valuable orders may be at stake, and also in public administration, where the public may become indignant if they believe that a public servant is 'getting above his station'.

We must also try to be aware of the person or persons to whom we are writing, selecting words carefully and considering the vocabulary we can take for granted in the person with whom we are corresponding. There are many immigrant members of our community who, while having a perfectly adequate 'working' knowledge of English, may be confused by colloquial expressions or figures of speech. Even a highly-educated native English speaker will have difficulty in understanding a letter which contains technical terms or 'jargon' peculiar to one specific area of business or administration.

Exercise 2.4. Write the letters requested:

(*a*) You are employed in the Rates Section of the City Treasurer's Department, and it has been decided by your new Departmental Head that the duplicated letters sent out to householders whose payments are in arrears are out of date in the English style they employ, and could even be interpreted by some sensitive ratepayers as impolite. You have been asked, therefore, to draft three new letters, to be sent when the rates are one month, two months and three months in arrears. (Remember that these are *duplicated* letters, and that the amounts involved, and other particulars, will be different in each case.)

(*b*) Frazer, Brown and Frazer, who have been good customers of yours for many years, owe £600. Draft three letters to be sent out when the amount has been outstanding for (i) six weeks; (ii) ten weeks; and (iii) three months.

Exercise 2.5. Here is an example of a very badly written letter, in terms of both the conventions of letter-writing and the 'tone' employed. First re-write Mr Thompson's letter for him, employing a suitable 'tone' and making sure that all the conventions are observed, and then write a reply based on the information given below the letter, in the *Note from your superior officer.*

27 Glenbourn Road
Newtown
NT2 3FF

27.5.80

Housing Dept
Newtown Corporation
High Street
Newtown
NT1 2PX

Sir,

I feel it's about time your dept attended to business for a change and sent me a cheque for the mortgage you promised me a month ago. I don't know what you lot do all day to earn those big salaries we poor ratepayers have to stump up for - drink tea I suppose - but I do know that I have all my stuff packed ready to move out, and I can't until I get that cheque. So when are you going to get a move on?

Yours

J. D. Thompson

Mr J.D. Thompson

Note from your superior officer

The property referred to is 'The Willows', 17 Ashford Crescent. On 15 March the property was inspected by our surveyor, Mr J. Rafferty. His report stated that although it was in poor repair the house was basically sound. He valued it at £9 500, subject to a list of repairs being carried out. The main items on the list were replacement of timbers affected by rot in the attic, renewing lead around certain windows and exterior painting. On 22 March this report was forwarded to the Committee which considered the matter at its April meeting and agreed to a mortgage if the listed repairs were carried out. A letter to that effect was sent to Mr Thompson on 17 April. Since then there is no record of any communication from him until now.

Exercise 2.6. Read the following letter A, and the note B, and write the reply requested:

A.

56 Richmond Road,
Belleway.
BE6 6JK

22nd May, 1980.

Dear Sir or Madam,

I am writing to say how annoyed I am about something that happened to me last week. I called in at your Office on Thursday at 2.30 p.m. because I had received a letter from you which stated that I should come and see one of your employees. When I arrived, I was sent up to the fifth floor and told to wait. A young woman came out to see me and asked me what I wanted, and when I told her she asked me to wait again and when she came back after fifteen minutes she said the person who was dealing with my case was out and I would have to come back another time.

This was very inconvenient for me and I am very annoyed about it. I spent 90p on the bus fare into town and out again, and all for nothing. I could understand it if I'd called in the lunch hour or after 5 o'clock, but surely in an office where you deal with the public it is your duty to make sure that someone is available to meet the public when they arrive. You didn't say anything in your letter about only coming at a certain time.

To make matters worse, before I went up to the fifth floor the porter insisted on looking in my shopping bag. I found this most distasteful, and look forward to receiving your comments on the whole unpleasant affair.

Yours faithfully,

Edna J. Williams

EDNA J. WILLIAMS (Mrs)

B. Note from your employer:

I knew this would happen sooner or later if we went over to flexitime; you'd better write her a letter apologising for the inconvenience caused, but you can point out politely that she could have rung up and made an appointment. Explain about our new system of flexible working hours and say that as our work is so specialised it isn't always possible for someone else to deal with the enquiry.

As far as the incident with the porter is concerned, I don't think she has a legitimate complaint. We *have* to be careful about security with all the bomb scares that occur nowadays. Unless he was discourteous, which I can't imagine, he was only doing his job.

Exercise 2.7. You are given the following letter A, which has been sent to your office, and the instructions B. Write the letter requested.

A.

186 Swallow Street,
Longton.

2nd October, 1980.

Dear Sir,

I am in receipt of your extremely discourteous communication concerning non-payment of rates. May I inform you that when I received my Rate Demand Notice last April I immediately applied to you for a reduction in rates. £270 a year is ridiculous and an unrealistic amount to pay for the privilege of living in the middle of a wasteland of dereliction in a two-room flat.

I paid half the amount demanded in June and have no intention of paying any more until something is done about the amount I am overcharged. May I point out that since I moved here in 1977 all the shops have been pulled down, the bus service is even worse than it was and I have no children to send to council schools so I'm getting nothing for my rates.

I hope to hear from you what you are going to do about this disgraceful state of affairs.

Yours faithfully,

Gerald Connolly.

GERALD CONNOLLY

B. Please acknowledge this letter. He must mean the final reminder we sent him last week. We have no record of a complaint from him but in any case tell him that we are not responsible for fixing rateable values. If he wants a revaluation he will have to apply to the Rating Valuation Officer for his district on form R.1—send him the form with your letter; the address to send it to will be on it.

His rates have already been reduced because of the state of the area—the amount is clearly set out on the Rate Demand Notice. The bus service has nothing to do with us. And what do you think he wants us to do about his non-existent children? Be tactful, but make it clear he will be in trouble if he doesn't pay by the end of this month. A plea for lower valuation pending is no excuse.

Internal Memoranda

When we wish to communicate with a person working within the same organisation as ourselves, the correspondence takes a different form from that sent outside. Many firms and organisations have their own 'memorandum' forms, specially printed for this purpose, and you should study the forms you come across in your own place of work.

Because memoranda are not usually sent through the post, they do not carry the address of the sender, nor do they require the address to which they are being sent. In most cases they bear the name of the organisation, and spaces to be filled in with the names and departments or sections of the sender and the recipient. A typical form would look something like this:

Trimfield District Council

Internal Memorandum

From:......................	To:......................
Dept:......................	Dept:......................

Here is another example, showing a slightly different form:

GREATER BURCHESTER COUNCIL

INTERDEPARTMENTAL MEMORANDUM

FROM TO

YOUR REF........ OUR REF......... TEL.EXT.NO...... DATE........

Having filled in the details provided for at the top of the form, you do not need to employ a salutation before beginning the body of the communication. What is almost always employed, however, is a subject heading, so that the correspondence begins like this:

WESTBROOK CORPORATION

Internal Memorandum

From: A. Trimby Stationery	**To:** J. Jones Solicitors Dept

Your Ref. MJ7/E **Our Ref.** 1927 **Date** 5/4/80

Re-ordering of Items in Regular Use

We wish to draw your attention to the new system for ordering items required on a regular basis.

It is not usual for a memorandum to be signed at the end. Some organisations like their employees to initial them, and some rely entirely upon the 'From' at the top, together with the reference, to locate the sender. This will depend on whether the matter dealt with is the direct responsibility of the writer, or whether the memorandum is written or typed by a junior member of the department on behalf of the person whose name appears at the top of the form.

Although a memorandum may not *look* quite as formal as a letter, it is just as important to communicate meaning as clearly and concisely as possible, and for this purpose it is essential to write in complete sentences.

Exercise 2.8. You receive the following memorandum from your Departmental Head. Write your reply on a suitably designed form:

<u>Proposed Introduction of Flexi-Time</u>

As you are aware, it has been proposed that this Department should adopt a system of flexible working hours. Certain difficulties have been envisaged, however, in ensuring that the needs of the public would be served if employees were free to choose their own hours of work. Perhaps you could think the matter over and let me have any constructive ideas that occur to you.

Exercise 2.9. There is trouble, not for the first time, over car parking at Southdown College of Further Education. The available space, which is reserved for staff, is a short distance from the College and unsupervised; too many people for one reason or another park close to the college building and make delivery of goods difficult. Also, the car park has a narrow entrance which is easily blocked by careless parking, so that part-time staff arriving after 9 a.m. sometimes cannot get in, or those wishing to leave early cannot get out, or there are no spaces left. Write a memorandum to all staff, asking them to use the car park and not to leave cars near the front or back doors, even for short periods, to display the stickers which show their right to park in the college car park, and to give the Vice-Principal a note of the numbers of their cars in case they have to be asked to move them.

Exercise 2.10. Having been approached by some of your colleagues with a view to setting up a sports club, you have decided to find out how much support there would be for such a venture. Write a suitable memorandum, including a tear-off strip on which people can indicate what they think of the idea. (Remember that once the strip is torn off, people may not keep the other half of your form.)

Exercise 2.11. Read the following note from the Head of your Department, and draft the memorandum requested:

> Something will have to be done to try to economise in this building. Can you therefore compose a memorandum to be sent to all members of staff, suggesting, for a start, ways of making the use of the telephone more economical? It's cheaper to phone after one o'clock, of course, and it's also cheaper to phone once to a place instead of several times a day with lots of little enquiries. I think a lot of money is wasted with people 'hanging on' instead of asking the person at the other end to call them back. And private calls *must* be cut out from now on. Post charges are so high now that we must avoid sending lots of little letters to the same address. I'm sure that, for instance, we could put the small, individually addressed envelopes into a larger one, which could be sealed and sent off each night. Another thing which people have become rather careless about is leaving lights on all over the place. I hope we can do something about this before the bill for electricity becomes insupportable.

3

Summary and Interpretation

Cutting out unnecessary words

We can save a great deal of time and money by using only the words that we really need to communicate our meaning. Most people's vocabularies include many words which can effect great economies if they are employed sensibly. For example:

> George has spent no less than ten years studying the science of supplying water to otherwise arid lands for the purpose of crop cultivation.

can become:

> George has spent a decade studying irrigation.

The second version of the sentence presents exactly the same information as the first, but much more *concisely. Conciseness* should be one of the main aims of communication. Consider the following sentence, and see how concisely you can re-write it:

> The man who had been employed to investigate the crime did not believe the excuse made by the person he suspected of having committed it that he had not been on the spot at the time.

Exercise 3.1. Re-write the following as concisely as possible:

(*a*) The boy was very successful in his attempts to solve the problem on account of the fact that he had attempted similar problems on many previous occasions.
(*b*) We will achieve a more satisfactory result if we work in association with each other.
(*c*) Making a full inventory of the stocks held in our warehouse is necessary before we can assess our ability to meet orders for goods to be sent out of the country for sale abroad.
(*d*) Kindly refrain from interjecting remarks and statements which do not bear any relation to the subject under discussion, as interruptions of this kind have the effect of appearing to have been introduced for the purpose of provoking hilarity.

(*e*) Tautology is the expression employed to denote the usage of superfluous words and phrases which do not add anything new to what has already in effect been stated in another form.
(*f*) Before issuing a signature in regard to goods arriving in response to earlier requests, employees should make a careful perusal of the statement of quantities and prices accompanying any such deliveries.

If you succeeded in considerably reducing the number of words in each of these sentences, you are well on the way to mastering the art of precis writing.

Précis writing

In business and public administration it is essential to be able to present the main points of a case or an argument as clearly and concisely as possible. While the details may be necessary at certain stages of negotiations, a well-written summary is often called for when the matter passes to another department or committee. And while examples and comparisons are sometimes useful in clarifying and explaining, they can be time-wasting and irritating to someone who is already familiar with the procedures involved.

How can we cut down the length of a piece of writing without sacrificing any of its essential meaning?

The first step in successful précis writing is simply *reading*. The passage may be a simple one, or it may be more complex. You may be able to grasp the essentials of what the writer is saying after one careful reading, or you may need to read it two or three times. When you *think* you have understood, you can test yourself by summing up the whole passage in one sentence. I find it useful to underline what I consider to be the main points, or changes of theme, in the passage, and then summarise each of these points or turns of thought in my own words.

When you are *certain* that you have thoroughly understood the passage, you can start to make notes *in your own words* of what you want to say in your new, shorter version. It is never enough simply to leave out some of what the author says; the only successful kind of précis is the one that is written from notes, just like an essay.

When you think you have a sufficient set of notes from which to construct your final version, it is as well to *check the number of words*. If it looks as if you are going to have too many, how can you achieve conciseness?

There are several ways of doing this, and you should check to see which of them can be most useful to you in the present situation:

(*a*) All restatements and repetitions can be cut out.
(*b*) Figures of speech can usually be dispensed with.

(*c*) Examples can be cut down. One is usually enough, especially if it is a well-chosen one.
(*d*) Any digressions from the essential theme of the passage can go.
(*e*) There are usually instances where the author has used a number of words instead of one. Single words substituted for long phrases can make a great difference.
(*f*) Do make *absolutely sure* that you have not inadvertently added any ideas of your own to those expressed in the passage.

You should now be ready to write your final version, keeping it concise and within the word limit set, but at the same time being careful to write grammatically in complete sentences and only dividing the material into paragraphs if it really needs it. A passage of 900 words may need to be divided into three paragraphs, whereas this may not be necessary for a 300 word summary.

To summarise the method:

Read; *check* understanding.
Divide; *check* each section.
Select; *check* your selections and omissions.
Make notes; *check* number of words.
Write; *check* sense, grammar, paragraphs.

Exercise 3.2. Reduce the following to about one-third of its present length:

It is true that when we attend an interview for a post, the person who interviews us will be most interested in finding out about our qualifications, our relevant experience (if we have any) and our ability to cope with the responsibilities the post involves. However, there are other factors which need to be taken into consideration when we are preparing ourselves to attend such an interview. Not the least important of these factors is our appearance. Many young people of today are interested in, and adept at, following the dictates of fashion. Those who have been working and earning money for some time are often skilled at presenting themselves in the most amazing varieties of fancy dress. And very impressive they look, too. But we have to remember that packaging is important, and whereas the 'Teddy Boy' or 'Punk Rock' styles may be ideally suited to the discotheque, they may not be calculated to appeal to the employer who is seeking a young person to represent his company at the reception desk, or to promote his product or service. Pink caps, green satin jeans, shaggy fur boots and lace overcoats no doubt have their place, but it is not in the office, and you may find it to your advantage to present an appearance which is rather less noticeable when you turn up for the interview for that all-important job.

Exercise 3.3. Make a précis of the following passage in not more than 230 words and supply a suitable title:

The staff of six special schools in the Manchester area were asked for their views on further education for the handicapped. Three schools replied, and the questions, with summaries of the responses, are set out below. Of the three respondent schools, one catered for the physically-handicapped, one for the hearing-impaired, and one for the partially-sighted.

The first question asked how far teachers thought that pupils either benefited or suffered from the effects of segregation in special schools. The view held by all respondents was that benefits outweigh any suffering under the present system. It was felt that while pupils educated in a special school environment may suffer from being deprived of the company of their non-handicapped peers, in the case of certain severe handicaps (profound deafness was mentioned) this segregation is unavoidable. It was felt that the alternative, of 'leaving the handicapped pupil at the mercy of teachers who . . . are untrained in the special skills required' is likely to hinder his education and development to an even greater degree. The general feeling was summed up by one respondent as 'In theory integration superior, in practice inferior', as it was felt that 'there is nobody more "segregated" than a solitary handicapped child struggling to manage in an ordinary school, without the necessary independence and confidence'. For this reason it was considered 'far better for them to start off in special schools, where expert help gives them the ability, the confidence and the initiative to take their place successfully later in ordinary schools'.

We next asked what proportion of students leaving special schools went on to 'integrated' establishments of further or higher education. Eight out of sixty-seven leavers had gone on from the physically handicapped school since its opening; twenty-three per cent of leavers from the hearing-impaired school ('mainly in connection with apprenticeships', implying part-time courses in FE); and approximately two per cent of the partially-sighted.

The next question asked whether there were many pupils who could benefit from going to FE colleges, but who did not get the opportunity. All respondents felt that there were some, and one respondent laid the blame for this situation at the doors of the colleges who 'cannot or will not cope with their difficulties'.

We next asked what could be done by colleges or local education authorities to improve this situation. One suggestion was 'the appointment of one person in the college with responsibility for supervising the few handicapped students involved and making himself aware of the special problems and needs which arise, and for liaising with representatives from the schools who are prepared to offer advice and for informing and advising the college teachers concerned'. Individual, additional tuition was seen as being a useful provision, as were extra Education or Welfare Department staff with special responsibility for supporting pupils going on to FE. Alternative suggestions involved bringing FE out of the colleges and into the schools, by the use of peripatetic teachers or special FE units attached to physically handicapped schools. These last suggestions, of course, completely miss the point of the social integration motive which prompted the enquiry in the first place. One respondent summed up the situation by saying 'Very little under present financial climate. Enormous backing resources in staff, materials and even buildings required for any hope of successful integration and progress'.

The last question asked what teachers thought of the idea of a 'special' college, such as Hereward College, Coventry, for the physically handicapped. One respondent thought the idea an excellent one, particularly if these share a campus with a normal college, as Hereward does with Tile Hill. It was felt to be essential, however, 'that staff should be drawn equally from those experienced with the physically handicapped as well as in FE'. It was pointed out that a general college for all handicaps would not have the same advantages as special colleges for particular handicaps, such as those run by the RNIB at Harbourne and Heathersett. Another respondent seemed to feel that support units for the handicapped within colleges were preferable to special colleges, and also put forward the idea of small hostels in areas with plenty of further education facilities, to cater for the needs of handicapped students from a wide area.

Exercise 3.4. Re-write the following letter, using not more than 200 words and expressing yourself clearly and simply:

Dear Sirs,

We are in receipt of yours of the 17th instant and beg to reply in the following terms.

We are amply aware of the difficulties you are experiencing in understanding the apparently disproportionate increases in the prices of the commodities with which we have been supplying you for a considerable period of time, and, we hope, to your complete satisfaction. The causes of these increases are to some extent rather complicated and we feel that in view of our long business association with you, you are entitled to some form of explanation, which we hope will go some way towards clarifying the situation and removing the causes of your dissatisfaction.

As you are no doubt aware, our costs in producing the materials with which we supply you originate in the main from two sources. Firstly there is the cost of raw materials, and secondly there is the cost of labour.

With regard to the first of these items, our expenses have increased steadily at intervals of six months throughout the period of our supplying you. However, being aware of the processes by which raw material prices increase, we generally make it our practice to hold stocks of raw materials, which in our case mainly refers to paper supplies, as far as is practicable in terms of storage space in our premises at the above address, in order to keep the price to our customers of the finished product as low as is practically possible. Thus you will see by perusing the invoices which we have submitted to you over the last twelve months, the prices of items ordered on a regular basis have been kept more or less constant over a period of time.

However, where items have not been re-ordered for some time, an increased material cost is often unavoidable, owing to the fact that your re-ordering has necessitated our buying in the paper on which to print your requirements at the increased prices currently being charged by our paper suppliers. We trust that this explanation is satisfactory.

With regard to labour costs, you will no doubt be aware that every year we are obliged to increase our wage bill. While we make every effort to absorb as much of this increased cost as we can, there is inevitably a certain proportion of the increase which has to be passed on to our customers.

We hope that the above explanation fully answers the points you raise in yours of the 17th instant, and trust that we may look forward to being of further service to you in the future and continuing the mutually advantageous relationship that our two companies have enjoyed in the past.

Yours faithfully,

Understanding the written word

The type of ingenuity required in condensing a long report into a few short paragraphs or reducing an unwieldy mass of correspondence to a concise set of notes depends heavily on our ability to understand another person's thought expressed in written form. This is often not very easy, and when difficulty arises it may be the writer's fault, if he has a bad style or misuses vocabulary, or it may be the reader's fault, if he is not giving his undivided attention to the task of reading, or if he is allowing his own views to stand in the way of understanding those expressed by the writer.

It is absolutely essential to read properly and carefully whatever is entrusted to us for interpretation. If you are not sure whether you understand something, try re-phrasing it in your own words. If you cannot do that to your own satisfaction, then you are not understanding it properly, and you need to seek help, either from a dictionary if it is only the odd word here and there that is causing difficulty, or from another person who knows more about the subject than you do.

As well as understanding the material to be condensed, the report, set of letters, or whatever it may be, you must be certain that you understand the instructions regarding what you are to do with it, so that you can carry them out *fully* and efficiently. You may, for instance, be asked simply to summarise a series of letters, or you may be asked, in addition, to write the next letter in the series.

Try to understand the motives of the writer, rather than simply interpret what he or she is saying in terms of words and punctuation marks only. Sometimes 'reading *between* the lines' can tell us more than what is actually written *on* the lines.

Exercise 3.5.

(*a*) Distinguish between the following pairs of words, writing sentences to bring out the differences in meaning:

neutral/indifferent	archaic/traditional
irritate/stimulate	briskly/hastily
pause/delay	carefree/casual
responsibility/right	warm/tepid
serious/solemn	approach/assault

(*b*) Give a word which means the opposite of each of these:

mature	similar	promptly	compulsory	diligent
real	harshly	lessen	superficial	benevolent

(*c*) Compose sentences to show the use of the following:

round as a noun; *round* as an adjective
that as a pronoun; *that* as an adjective
coin as a noun; *coin* as a verb

sleep as a noun; *sleep* as a verb
each as an adjective; *each* as a pronoun.

Exercise 3.6. Read the following passage carefully, and then answer the questions at the end:

The problem of women cannot be split off. Women cannot be separated from the whole working class. All social life and all political problems are first and foremost rooted in classes and class conflict, not in age, sex, nationality, religion or anything else. Very often the ruling class tries to swell our perception of the differences between sections of the class beyond all proportion, in order to pit one section of the working class against another. Women form just such a section. Everybody knows that throughout the world women suffer discrimination. But it is important to recognise the ideology which encourages and needs such discrimination not as the ideology of the male sex but of the ruling class. Such discrimination is an attack upon the whole working class for two reasons: there is the cheapening of labour power by the sheer abuse of women, and the fact that many women go out to work is used by employers as an excuse to pay their menfolk less than a breadwinner's wage. Women will never be free without the emancipation of their class.

Out of the 25 million workers in this industrial country, more than one third are women. Capitalism here would die without these wage slaves. There is no such thing as equal pay in Britain. Even in those sectors of workers—teachers, civil servants, medical workers—where allegedly there is equal pay, women do not have the same opportunities. Higher skills, free choice of vocation, advancement in any trade or profession are barred to them.

The woman at home cannot be ignored as if she was divorced from politics. She is a member of the working class, highly skilled yet not paid by capitalism. She scrimps and saves to make her husband's meagre wage go round—feeding and looking after today's wage slaves, producing and bringing up tomorrow's. In effect, her husband's boss pays one wage and gets two workers for it. So the housewife is a vital part of the working class. She is the one who sees how small the wage packet is in relation to the food and clothes her family needs. She knows where her loyalty lies—with her working husband and children against the boss. Her family look to her for support when they go on strike or occupy the factories, for without her cooperation they know they're lost. Wives who do not stand by their husbands in the class struggle are deluded as to where their real interests lie.

Since 1960 there has been a marked trend appearing in the working lives of women: the majority of women return to work at about the age of 30, after a short period of child raising; 55 per cent of working women are still working in the peak child-caring years of 25–29. And yet the bulk of recent educational expansion has taken place in the field of science and technology, in courses where boys have always outnumbered, and still outnumber, girls.

Under socialism husbands and families are expected and encouraged to play their full part in the running of the home. Work shifts and transport are organised to suit the needs of women workers. Having a baby does not destroy a woman's career as it usually does in Britain. When she is able, she can return to her career without loss. Working women and children are helped by the development of nurseries at the place of work.

(*a*) Supply a suitable title for this passage.
(*b*) In not more than 60 of your own words, summarise the writer's argument in the first paragraph.
(*c*) What is meant by the expression 'breadwinner' (line 12)?
(*d*) 'Such discrimination is an attack upon the whole working class for

two reasons' (lines 9–10). In two sentences, state in your own words what the writer holds the two reasons to be.

(*e*) In line 5, the writer refers to 'sections of the class'. What is meant by this?

(*f*) From paragraph two, choose one statement which you think is objective and one which you think is subjective, and explain the difference between them.

(*g*) In not more than 50 of your own words, state what you understand the writer to be saying in paragraph three.

(*h*) What is meant by the expression 'occupy the factories' (line 28)?

(*i*) What is the relationship between the first and second sentences in paragraph four?

(*j*) What is 'technology' (line 35)?

(*k*) What sort of publication do you think this extract was taken from? Give reasons for your answer.

(*l*) Write about 100 words on the theme 'Women in the Modern World'.

Exercise 3.7. Here is a business letter written from one company to another. Note that the 'house style' here is different from the letters which have been reproduced up to this point. This 'blocked' style is considered by many firms to be more modern than the older 'indented' style. Read all the information given in the letter and the memorandum, and answer the questions that follow.

Corrugated Containers Ltd

Mill Lane,
Wolverhampton,
WV4 7FX

3 March 1980

Mr M. Hart
Manager
Braden & Co (Printers) Ltd
BIRMINGHAM
B6 7BA

Dear Mr Hart,

I have now received delivery of several of the items of stationery I ordered from you in December, together with your invoice for £872.67 plus VAT.

I am sorry to have to tell you that I am far from satisfied with the end product. You will recall that when you first came to visit me back in September, you agreed that although it was not your usual practice, you would have all the stationery I ordered printed to my detailed specifications. On this understanding, you quoted prices for the various items, which I accepted. I did express to you at the time my surprise at the magnitude of some of the prices.

However, in view of the fact that your Company had been so warmly recommended to me by Mr Lawrence Parker of Wolverhampton Laundries Ltd, I decided that it was worth paying your somewhat higher prices for the privilege of being sure of getting what I wanted. As I explained to you at the time, I felt this to be particularly important in view of the fact that we are setting up a new Company and wish to present the best possible 'image' to potential customers.

I am far from satisfied with the stationery now that it has finally arrived. In spite of the fact that I specified the type-styles and spacing that were to be used on all items, I find that you have varied it on some of them (i.e. the Internal Memorandum forms). In addition, the invoice sets, which I was particularly at pains to design exactly to my requirements, are nearly three-quarters of an inch shorter than the length I specified. I must admit that in other respects the work is well done.

However, on perusing your invoice, I find that the prices I have been charged are well in excess of what I was quoted. Quite apart from the VAT, which I had understood to be included, some of the prices for the items themselves have been increased. I am at a loss to understand how you can explain this, particularly in view of the fact that you demanded a payment of £200 on account when I placed the order in December.

I hope that you will look into these complaints at once and issue a credit note for the cost of the Internal Memorandum forms (£20) and the Invoice sets (£160) and the excess charge, which I estimate to be in the region of £120.

Yours sincerely,

S. Wrench

S. Wrench

MEMORANDUM

FROM: M. Hart, Manager DATE: 6.3.80

TO: S. Martin, Director

Subject: Corrugated Containers Ltd

Mr Wrench had his stationery delivered last Thursday, and since it was the last day of the month, his invoice went out with it. You will remember that he is the man I went to see in Dovedale Park, starting up a new business making corrugated packaging.

We have been particularly careful to keep to his instructions, which were written out in great detail and included things like how many millimetres from the top of the page the printing was to start. Everything except the memos was submitted to him at the proof stage, and he made alterations to some of the items then. I did ask the typist to show the additional cost for these alterations quite clearly on the invoice, along with my original quoted price, but I have now seen the file copy, and probably because she was in a hurry to get the invoice out with the goods, she didn't do it.

The Internal Memos were the only item for which he didn't ask for a proof. He showed me a copy but didn't let me bring it away, so I just had them printed in the usual house style. As regards the Invoice Sets, I warned him from the beginning that there would be difficulties in getting an eleven-part set to stick together. This is what happened, and the finishing department had to trim the tops off and try again with a stronger glue. Perhaps we could allow him something for that, but since he didn't ask for a proof of the Memos, I'm not prepared to take them back.

I know some of this is my fault. I should have sent him a written statement of the additional charges for his alterations, and also put in writing that VAT would be added. But I expected a businessman to know that.

Questions

1. Decide what you—as Mr Martin, the Director—are going to do about Mr Wrench's letter, and write a reply to be signed by Mr Hart.
2. Compose a memorandum to be sent to all departments which will help to ensure that such situations will not recur.

Summary of correspondence

Précis-writing takes on a particular significance for us when we have to reduce a series of letters to a simple piece of prose writing. This could be necessary, for instance, when the correspondence is being passed to a lawyer for advice, or when a summary is to be placed before a committee for its consideration. It is quite easy to find ways of reducing the length of letters, since much of the introductory and concluding material will inevitably be dictated more by politeness and convention than by the needs of communication. We should remember, however, that chronological order needs to be kept, and that *dates* can be of primary importance. Many words can be saved by composing a good *title,* giving the full names and addresses of the parties to the correspondence and indicating the subject.

Paragraphing is also important. It makes a lot of sense to have a new paragraph for each letter. You should certainly not try to keep the number of paragraphs within each of the individual letters you are summarising, as many of these will disappear in your shorter versions.

Remember that the summary should be in *reported speech*: 'I', 'me', 'you', 'we' and 'us' in the letters will become third-person pronouns in the summary, and there will be corresponding changes in possessive adjectives. Verbs will all be in the past tense, and words such as 'today', 'this', and 'these' will have to be brought into line. Question marks will disappear.

Exercise 3.8. Make a summary of the following correspondence in not more than 170 words of continuous prose, and give it a suitable title. The summary will be used for reference in a Committee meeting where the case will be discussed.

Walker's Coal Merchants Limited

83 Bentley Street, Trimfield, TR1 0FX

1st March, 1980.

The City Estates and Valuation Office,
The Town Hall,
TRIMFIELD.
TR2 7LB

Dear Sir,

In response to your advertisement in the <u>Trimfield Chronicle</u> of 25th February, I am writing to ask for details about the land you are offering for sale at Wentworth Common.

We are particularly interested in knowing what the "planning permission" referred to in your advertisement covers.

If we were to purchase all or part of this land, we would mainly be using it as storage for coal and smokeless fuel, but would also be interested in the possibility of building a depot for the maintenance of our vehicles at a later date.

We would be grateful to receive your comments with details of the land offered at your earliest convenience.

Yours faithfully,

A. TRAVIS
Manager
Walker's Coal Merchants Ltd

Trimfield District Council

Estates and Valuation Department

Town Hall, Trimfield. TR2 7LB

5 March 1980

A. Travis Esq.
Manager
Walker's Coal Merchants Ltd
83 Bentley Street
TRIMFIELD TR1 0FX

Dear Sir,

Thank you for your letter of 1 March, inquiring about the land that the Council has for sale at Wentworth Common.

The land in question comprises four lots of four acres each, which the Council is prepared to sell either separately or in one lot. At present three of the lots are unoccupied. Two are entirely free of buildings, but there is a row of six derelict cottages on one site. These cottages were condemned as unfit dwellings in 1971, but it would be possible for a purchaser to renovate them if the proposed plans were passed by the District Council. The fourth part of the land is partly occupied by Council allotments, the leases on which are due to lapse in 1981, when they will not be renewed. The price of the land is £10 000 per acre. A proportion of the rent of the allotments would be paid by the Council to any purchaser of that part of the land. There is no additional price for the derelict cottages. As a result of a previous application, the Council granted planning permission for a storage depot for refrigerated vehicles, but as the area is predominantly a residential one, it was felt inadvisable to grant permission for petrol pumps and an automatic vehicle washing machine.

I hope that this information will be of assistance to you, but please do not hesitate to write to us again, should you have any further enquiries.

Yours faithfully

E.D. BARNWELL
Chief Valuation Officer

Walker's Coal Merchants Limited

83 Bentley Street, Trimfield, TR1 OFX

10th March, 1980.

The City Estates and Valuation Office,
The Town Hall,
TRIMFIELD.
TR2 7LB

Dear Sir,

Thank you for your letter of 5th March, giving details of the land for sale at Wentworth Common.

We are interested in purchasing at least part of the land, but before proceeding further we should like to know whether planning permission for altering the six cottages you refer to would be dependent upon their continuing to be used as residences. Or might it be possible to convert them into offices?

Also, we wonder whether it might be possible for us to buy the three vacant lots now, and perhaps obtain some agreement that we could have "first refusal" on the remaining land when the lease on the allotments runs out?

Yours faithfully,

A. TRAVIS

Manager,
Walker's Coal Merchants Ltd

Exercise 3.9. Turn to Exercise 2.4, page 18, and write summaries of the letters you wrote in (*a*) and (*b*), reducing them to about one-third of their present length.

Exercise 3.10. Summarise in the same way your correspondence with
(*a*) Mr Thompson (Exercise 2.5, pages 18–19)
(*b*) Mrs Williams (Exercise 2.6, pages 19–20)
(*c*) Mr Connolly (Exercise 2.7, page 21).

4

Essays

Ever since your primary school days you have been setting down your thoughts and opinions on paper in the form of essays or 'compositions'. By the time you left school you may have been thoroughly bored with the exercise. On the other hand, if you are of a creative or literary turn of mind—the kind of person who is described as being 'good at English'—expressing your own thoughts and feelings may be one of your greatest sources of satisfaction.

There are many forms of writing which come under the umbrella of 'original composition'. A letter to your friend is an obvious example. Articles on hobbies and interests, advertisements aimed at persuading people to buy something, travel agents' literature, stories, poems—all these require the same kind of thoughtful planning if they are to be coherent and interesting to the reader.

What sort of composition are you going to write?

There are a number of 'modes' you can adopt, depending on the subject you have been given to write about.

Descriptive writing paints a picture in words of the subject.
Expository, or explanatory, writing takes this a stage further and helps the reader to understand the topic or subject.
Argumentative writing looks closely at both sides of an argument or issue and weighs them against each other before reaching a carefully-considered conclusion. This is the kind of essay which is often expected in examinations, and it is easier to make out a good case for your side by presenting the arguments against it first, and then setting out the counter-arguments more strongly before arriving at your conclusion.
Critical writing makes a study of something which has been written or spoken by another person or group of people and evaluates it.
Narrative writing tells a story.
Persuasive writing aims to get someone to do something, go somewhere, buy something, or stop doing something.

Of course, many compositions will combine more than one of these 'modes'. Expository and critical work has to employ a certain amount of description. A story may well contain a large proportion of descriptive writing. An argument may be persuasive, and we may aim to persuade by means of an argument.

How do you choose what you should write about?

If you are simply given a subject and told to get on with writing two or three pages, your only problem is to decide which of the 'modes' just enumerated will give you most scope for expressing your ideas and exercising your talents, but sometimes you are asked to write 'on *one* of the following', and then the choice is more complicated.

You should try to decide which of the topics or subjects is most interesting to you. The more interested you are, the more chance there is of your being able to communicate that interest to your readers. Obviously you will have to know a certain amount about the subject. It is all very well to feel intuitively convinced that 'Plato's Theory of Knowledge' is a more interesting topic than 'Sardines', but it may be much more difficult to find two or three pages to write about it.

If you know that you are a very talented story-teller, or have a gift for presenting a logical and well-balanced argument, you should look for the topic which will enable you to use that talent.

Having chosen the subject, what do you do next?

The short answer to this is: decide what you are going to say, and how you are going to say it. You make a *plan,* according to the following formula:

(*a*) Jot down everything you want to say, in any order, to see whether there is going to be enough of it. It is better to get any false starts over with at this stage, before wasting too much time.
(*b*) Group together the ideas that seem to you to go together.
(*c*) Put them in the order in which you think it will be best to present them.
(*d*) Decide how you are going to begin, how you will introduce your subject, remembering that first impressions are important since you are hoping to inspire your readers with a desire to see what else you have to say.
(*e*) Decide how you are going to finish your essay. You must finish, and not merely stop as if the allotted time had run out and someone had wrenched the pen from your hand. The most impressive way of concluding is by evaluating what you have said, summing it up, and referring back in some way to either your title or your opening sentence.

The different ways in which a topic can be approached are illustrated by the following notes made by four students when faced with the one-word title 'Advertising':

Student A

A man in a pub, telling his friend about what a good time he had on a recent coach outing—'We sang all the songs we knew—Watney's, Esso, Typhoo, Beanz Meanz Heinz—the lot!'
Question—can we ever persuade people to do/buy anything unless they are already willing to be persuaded?

Student B

For:

1. Advertising creates demand, therefore employment for people making the product.
2. It increases competition, and makes competing manufacturers more concerned to market a better product at a lower price.
3. Makes shopping easier by informing consumers of what is available.
4. 'Legal, decent, honest, truthful'—if an advertiser's goods don't come up to his claims, you can get him.

Against:

1. The cost of advertising is added to the final cost of the product.
2. Built in obsolescence—people buy new to 'keep up with the Jones's' when they might go on using consumer durables they already have.
3. It only shows the good points of things.
4. Bad for children, e.g. spelling 'Beanz', 'Pinta' etc.

Student C

Advertising—how does it work?

1. Appeals to snobbery—'Top people', etc.
2. " " sociability—'You can't beat 'em'
3. " " fear (the converse of 1 and 2 above)
4. The big S—'All because the lady likes . . .'

Student D

Kinds of advertising: *Press, T.V., leaflets, cinema, etc. Also sports sponsorship.*
Methods employed: Slogans, 'unsolicited testimonials', famous people, free offers, bargains, etc.

A note on paragraphing

Sometimes people feel a little confused about what a paragraph should be like. They wonder how long to make them, or how many paragraphs an essay of, say, three pages, should contain. This is really a very simple matter. When you make a plan for an essay, you will have a number of points, or groups of related points. You will also have decided on the order in which you are going to present these points. So why not let each of them constitute a paragraph? That takes care of the number question.

As for length, a paragraph which consists of one sentence, baldly stating the point you wish to make, will not necessarily be an interesting one. It will prove either that the point itself is trivial and unworthy of much attention, or that you do not know enough about it. A good paragraph will develop your idea thoroughly, and this development will dictate its own length. Practice will enable you to vary the structure, or 'shape' of your paragraphs, so that you can sometimes employ a statement-discussion-conclusion structure, sometimes give lots of examples or 'cases' which will lead up to your statement of opinion towards the end, and sometimes state your point somewhere in the middle of the paragraph, with examples and discussion on both sides.

If you really do find this difficult, you can always adopt the expedient of making a little plan for each paragraph individually, taking the points one-by-one from your essay-plan proper and working out how you are going to develop each of them. This method seems to help those people whose essays tend to be too short. Like any other skill, this becomes second nature after a while.

Try to link your paragraphs by making a reference at the end of one or the beginning of the next to what will be or has just been said.

Exercise 4.1. Choose *one* of the following titles, state what *kind* of essay you are writing (narrative, descriptive, etc.), make a careful *plan,* and then write *two to three pages* of your own ideas on the subject:

(*a*) The problems of old age
(*b*) My home town
(*c*) Trade Unions and the modern world
(*d*) Smoking can damage your health
(*e*) Money
(*f* The freedom of the press
(*g*) Family life
(*h*) Women's place is . . .?
(*i*) Fact is stranger than fiction
(*j*) 'Politics is the art of the possible'

Exercise 4.2. The College staff are planning next year's educational trips and they would like you to write an article of 200–250 words describing what you would expect to gain from going on such a trip. Each trip will last no longer than a week and the suggestions which have been made so far are as follows: a fishing trip, a pony trek, a walking or climbing trip, a tour of London, a boating holiday. You may, however, have an idea of your own, but remember that finance is limited. The best articles will be circulated to all the students to give them an idea of the possibilities. The staff are interested to know what you expect to learn, as well as what you expect to enjoy.

Exercise 4.3.

(*a*) Choose one of the topics listed under Exercise 4.1, and plan the essay you would write.
(*b*) Write (i) the opening paragraph; and (ii) the conclusion.

Exercise 4.4. Write three paragraphs on themes from the above list. In your first paragraph state your theme at the outset and then develop it; in the second state the theme in the middle of the paragraph; and in the third lead up gradually to a statement of the theme at the end.

Exercise 4.5. Turn back to the students' notes on page 40, choose one set of notes, and write the essay that you think he or she would have written from the notes.

Exercise 4.6. Examine the following set of notes made collectively by a class of students when faced with the essay topic 'Women's Rights', and then answer the questions at the end.

```
Women's Rights

1.  Pay - equal pay for equal work?
      N.B. Manipulation of job specifications.

2.  Job security - is maternity leave enough?
                 - what about paternity leave?

3.  Does this influence  (a)  women's role expectation?
                         (b)  their employment prospects?
                         (c)  their education?

4.  Roles in the employment situation - should there ever
    be specifically 'male' and 'female' jobs?  Cf. chefs
    v. canteen ladies, domestic science teachers, ship's
    captains etc.
       N.B. Would you work for (under) a woman?

5.  Roles in the home - are they reversible - why?-
    why not?
       N.B. Why shouldn't the one with more earning
            power be the breadwinner?
            Have women any more right than men to be idle?
```

6. Insurance - no money for husband and children when bread-winning wife is out of work - husband expected to find work -does not apply the other way round.

7. Mortgages, Hire purchase etc.

Questions

(*a*) Make three lists from the above notes, of (i) factors which you feel could be discussed in an expository essay; (ii) points more suited for an argumentative essay; and (iii) those points which could be used in a persuasive piece of writing.

(*b*) Write *one* of the above three essays.

(*c*) Exchange essays with another member of the class and write an essay criticising the exposition, argument, or persuasion which he or she has produced.

5

Oral Communication

Imagine that you arrive at work one day and find the following memorandum on your desk:

INTERNAL MEMORANDUM

FROM: Chief Personnel Officer **TO:** B.E.C. Student.

DATE: 11/2/80

Local Radio Broadcasting

We have received an invitation from the local radio station to take part in a series of programmes dealing with employment in the city. As you have been here such a short time, we thought it might be a good idea for you to go along and talk on the radio about what you do and how you see your prospects.

Please let me know if you are willing to take part.

What would you do? If your answer is 'Panic!' or 'Hand in my notice', I sympathise. Most people are nervous about speaking in public anyway, but how much worse it would seem to be surrounded by strange faces and all kinds of complicated and unfamiliar electronic equipment.

But think again—isn't there in most of us a touch of the showman? Wouldn't you be a little bit envious if someone else had been chosen? And considered calmly, what does such an assignment really involve?

For a start, when we are going to communicate orally, whether we are speaking to one person on the telephone, a dozen in a departmental meeting, or twenty thousand on the radio, there is nothing to stop us working out on paper beforehand precisely what we are going to say.

Remember the planning strategy employed for written communication:

(*a*) The first thing you must do is to be sure what you are going to write about;
(*b*) having decided that, it is a good idea to write down all the thoughts that come into your head in connection with the subject;
(*c*) and see which of the ideas go together, and in what order they should be presented.

However, in the case of our broadcast, there is more involved than just communicating ideas or information. This is also an exercise in public relations. In addition to the points above:

(*a*) We need to state things clearly and simply, without jargon or specialist vocabulary;
(*b*) we need to employ an appropriate 'tone', civil and informative;
(*c*) we must interest the audience in what we have to say.

It stands to reason that oral communication which consists of someone reading out a piece of written communication is not going to be interesting to hear. It will sound stilted and unnatural and provoke the comment that 'People don't talk like that'. So once you have written your 'script' you will need to make adjustments to make your talk sound lively and natural, and to make you sound like a real person, and this means a friendly, helpful, sensible person who wants to give as much information as possible.

There is nothing to prevent you from practising what you want to say, and in fact you will have to do so if you are going to meet the time limit which will undoubtedly be imposed.

Because some people seem to have a natural gift for 'solo' performance, and others are better at working in groups, you may choose here between two alternative exercises. But remember that one bad 'performance' can let down the whole group, and that everyone at some time in his or her life has to speak for himself or herself.

Exercise 5.1—To be done alone. Write and tape-record a three-minute speech explaining to the citizens of your town either:

(*a*) What your Department or firm does; or
(*b*) Why you like your own job.

Exercise 5.2—Group assignment. Write and tape-record a five-minute 'programme' to be broadcast by your local radio station, explaining to the public the course that you are taking at college, what sort of people take it, and how it will benefit them in their careers.

Whether you are working alone or in a group, you should appoint another member of the class to act as your 'technician' and look after the tape-recording for you.

Taking notes

If we are to be able to write a lucid criticism of a broadcast talk, we must be able to listen carefully to what is being said, while at the same time making brief notes of the main points. Many people have difficulty when they first begin to take notes, because they try too hard to get down every word that the speaker or lecturer is saying, and of course they get hopelessly left behind. Others try to get by with just jotting down one-word headings and hoping that these will serve to remind them of what was said. Unfortunately most of our memories are too fallible for that to work, either.

However, note-taking is really a form of précis-writing, or summary. It requires exactly the same skills of pin-pointing the essentials of what is being said and not taking too much notice of the examples, illustrations and digressions the speaker uses to keep the attention of his or her audience, although if the general method employed is particularly good or particularly bad, this is certainly worth mentioning in the notes. Generally speaking, it will be necessary to indicate briefly at the end of your notes on the broadcast whether the talk or programme was satisfactory or not.

What makes oral communication satisfactory?

1. Having noted down *what* was said, there should be no difficulty in answering the question 'was the talk informative?' In other words, did it do what the instructions said it had to do—*explain*?
2. Did it present the information clearly, simply, without using specialist jargon?
3. Was it *interesting*? In particular, did it catch your attention from the start, make you want to go on listening? Or would you have switched off if this had come on your radio at home?
4. Were the examples used (if any) good ones? Did the speaker refer to specific local issues? After all, this was *local* radio.
5. Did it avoid saying anything that might hurt, upset or offend anyone listening, or result in a postbag of angry letters being delivered to the radio station?
6. *Could you hear it?* Did the presenter and performers speak clearly and avoid making noises of any kind which would distract attention from what they were saying?

Expanding your notes

When you come to expand your notes and incorporate your cryptic criticisms into a more formal and structured piece of writing, you should remember to write in continuous prose, as your criticisms will go unappreciated if they cannot be understood because of incomplete sentences or unintelligent punctuation.

In addition, although your notes may be one-line, or one-sentence, summaries of what was said, in the order in which it was said, followed by a critical comment at the end, you are at liberty to arrange your material as you wish when you re-write it. If you wish to give extra weight to the beginning, the middle or the end, this is up to you. And one or two paragraphs should be sufficient to criticise such a short broadcast.

Exercise 5.3.

(*a*) Listen carefully to the recordings of the 'talks and programmes' and make brief notes of the content of each. At the end of each broadcast you may take five minutes to add to your notes any critical comments you may wish to make.

(*b*) Choose *one* of the broadcasts and expand your notes on it into a short critical review of about 200–250 words. This should be suitable for publication in your local newspaper.

Exercise 5.4. Write a critical review, suitable for publication in a newspaper, of either a sporting event or a concert you have recently attended. You should employ a vocabulary suitable to your subject and your readership.

Exercise 5.5. You have been asked to give a talk on your hobby at your union's annual conference. Plan the talk and produce a set of notes to speak from. Do not write out the speech in full.

The use of the telephone

When we speak to somebody on the telephone, it is important for us to remember that he or she cannot see us, and therefore we must be careful to express what we have to say precisely, as we cannot rely on the nonverbal aids we use in face-to-face communication.

Because of this, and because of the expense of telephone calls, it is important to prepare in advance what we wish to say. If the message to be conveyed is a complex one, it is a good idea to make notes in advance, including any references, and dates of correspondence to which we may wish to refer.

In order to be heard properly, we must speak directly into the instrument and avoid turning away from it to consult notes or files or another person in the office. Never speak with anything in your mouth. Speak reasonably slowly, but avoid making unnatural pauses which would distort the meaning of what you are saying. It may be necessary to spell proper nouns such as personal names or trade marks, or technical words which may be unfamiliar to the listener.

When you are making business telephone calls, bearing in mind the following points will help to keep the cost to a minimum:

1. Whenever it is possible, ring after 1 p.m., when calls are cheaper.
2. Get into the habit of finding out whether there will be other calls needed to the same number during the course of the day. If you can, deal with all the enquiries or issues in one call.
3. When your call is answered, ask for the person to whom you want to speak. Give an extension number whenever possible, or state which Department you require.
4. If the person you want is not available, do not 'hang on'. Either leave your enquiry and a time at which you will call again, or request that the person should call you, giving your name and extension number and mentioning a time when you are sure you will be available.
5. Deal with your business as briefly as possible, while keeping your tone of voice friendly and courteous. The person on the other end of the line cannot see a smile, so try to let him or her hear one in your voice.
6. Have a pen or pencil and paper at the ready to take notes if necessary.
7. If you find you have dialled a 'wrong number', apologise and check the number you have obtained to avoid repeating the error.

When you are answering the telephone, give your name and the names of your office, section, department or firm. The use of 'Mr' is a mistake: a man should introduce himself as 'Alan Tucker', or whatever his name is. Women, on the other hand, can usefully indicate how they are addressed by introducing themselves as 'Miss Tucker' or 'Mrs Tucker'.

If the call is not for you, either take the caller's name and number so that he can be contacted when the person he wants returns, or offer a time when you know that person will be in the office. It is always a good idea to write down the caller's name as soon as it is mentioned, to avoid the embarrassment of admitting that you have forgotten it.

If the call is for you but is, for example, an enquiry which you cannot answer immediately, do not waste the caller's time and money by asking him to 'hang on', but state in a friendly way that it will take you a certain length of time to find the information he requires, and offer to telephone him as soon as it is available. Even if you fail to find a satisfactory answer, it is more courteous to ring back and say so, and request more time, than to let the caller think the enquiry is being ignored.

Whether an incoming call is for you or for one of your colleagues, it is very useful to keep a pad beside the telephone on which to note:

(*a*) the date and time of the call;
(*b*) the person for whom the caller asked;
(*c*) the caller's name, the name of the organisation he or she represents, the telephone number and extension;
(*d*) details of the message, including any relevant order numbers, references or dates;
(*e*) your name.

Many firms and organisations have specially-printed 'telephone message pads' for this purpose, and such printed forms are less likely to be lost or mislaid than miscellaneous little scraps of paper.

A final point to remember is that it is dishonest to use the office telephone for your personal calls unless you pay for them or have specific permission.

Telegrams and telex messages

These forms of communication carry the principles of précis to an extreme conclusion. They are expensive ways of communicating and should be used only when it is not practicable, because of the urgency of the message, to send a letter. For reasons of cost the normal rules of grammar are suspended in these cases and only the essential words are used. However, care must be taken when condensing to make sure that the message is still clear. The only punctuation that can be used in a telegram is the word 'stop' to separate groups of words and avoid possible misunderstandings.

Most large concerns have 'telegraphic addresses' consisting usually of the name of the organisation and the name of the town.

Examples of telegrams are as follows:

```
JACKSON  16 WEST STREET BOLTON
TRAIN CANCELLED UNABLE ARRIVE TUESDAY STOP MEET BOLTON
WEDNESDAY 8 AM WALTER
```

```
MANTAB RICHMOND
NO DELUXE AVAILABLE DO I SEND STANDARD LEWIS BROMLEY
```

Telegrams may be sent either by going to a Post Office and filling in a Telegram Form, of which a copy should be kept, or by telephone. The appropriate number to dial for sending telegrams can be found in the local telephone directory. It is important to write down exactly what you wish to say before making the call. The message should then be dictated slowly to the Operator, who will read it back. The date and time of the telephone call should be noted on the copy. It is usual to follow up a telegram by written confirmation in letter form, allowing for explanations and more normal phraseology.

Telex is the system by which organisations can communicate with each other by teleprinter. The machine records the message as it is typed and reproduces it immediately in exactly the same form at one or more points of reception. It is thus particularly valuable in dealing with urgent matters of a complicated or detailed nature. The terminal is, however, a very expensive mechanism and should be used with care.

Exercise 5.6. Make notes for a telephone call you are going to make to a technical college in another town, enquiring about courses similar to the one you are taking.

Exercise 5.7. Make notes for a telephone call to your central stationery stores, ordering your next month's requirements.

Exercise 5.8. Make notes for a telephone call to a local hotel, booking a room for a visiting speaker who is coming to address your debating society.

Exercise 5.9—Working in pairs. Act out the above conversations, with one person being the caller and the other answering the telephone.

Exercise 5.10. Write out the telegrams you would send in each of the following cases:

(*a*) Your employer has just telephoned to tell you that his car has been stolen from outside a restaurant, while he was on his way to see Mr George Edwards of 16 High Street, Bangor-on-Dee. He is stranded and has very little money on him, and asks you to telegraph to Mr Edwards, who is not on the telephone, to explain the position.

(*b*) Some stationery that you ordered three weeks ago and which should have been delivered by now has not arrived, and you need it urgently. The suppliers, Educational Books Ltd, Redland, Bristol 6, are not contactable by telephone, so you have to send a telegram.

Exercise 5.11. Write letters to the recipients of each of the telegrams in Exercise 5.10, confirming the messages.

6
Reports

There must have been occasions in your private and working life when you have been asked to consider the implications of some new idea or proposal. When you think over a matter carefully, make notes of your reactions, marshal these notes into a logical order and then write your reply, you are in effect writing a small, simple report.

Any report, whatever form it takes, must present the precise information asked for, in logical order, as concisely as possible, avoiding the use of specialist jargon. In addition, it must be presented attractively and laid out in a way that makes it easy for the reader to locate the particular information he or she is looking for, without having to wade through vast quantities of material. For this reason, it is useful and customary to divide the report into sections and to employ a system of headings and sub-headings to guide the reader through the report.

Different kinds of report

Perhaps the simplest and most familiar kind of report is the *eye-witness report* which gives an account of something that has taken place. You may have been asked at some time to fill in a form giving details of an incident you have witnessed or been involved in, for the use of the police or an insurance company.

What are the essential features of such a report? First of all, we are writing about something which has already taken place. It stands to reason that we can write a report only about something that has already happened. Therefore the report should be written in the *simple past tense,* just as the policeman, reading aloud from his notebook in court, will say 'I *was proceeding* down Warburton Road, when I *saw* . . .'.

Further reference to the policeman's notebook yields us our second principle: we must be *absolutely accurate* about dates, times, distances and dimensions. The sequence of events must be presented in strict *chronological order* if the report is to make sense.

We must remember that we are dealing with the purely *factual,* and there is no place in a report for the exercise of imagination or the expression of emotion.

Finally, we should supply a *title,* stating precisely what the report is about: what happened, where it happened, and when; and we must *sign* and *date* the report at the end.

Exercise 6.1. You have witnessed an incident which took place on an all-night bus and resulted in the driver calling the police on his radio-telephone. Write a report for use by the police, giving full details of what you saw and heard, with the relevant times and places.

Other kinds of report

Reports other than straightforward eye-witness reports involve the writer in collecting information from various sources and organising it into a coherent form.

Sources of information

Information is collected in many ways, ranging from inquiries made of individuals in a face-to-face situation, to the use of reference books and libraries. However, when a single individual is required to produce a report, he or she will not normally be expected to be an expert on complicated statistical sampling techniques. Common sense will indicate the kinds of ideas and information required by any particular report, and in general the sources of information likely to be found most useful are:

Personal investigation

There are many occasions when information can be obtained by simply going and having a good look at something. If, for example, a proposal has been made that your Company should move its premises to one of two or more new sites, you could visit the sites to find out for yourself what they have to offer. What kinds of districts are they situated in? Are there houses, shops, transport facilities nearby?

Asking questions

Closely linked to the 'see for yourself' technique is the practice of asking people what they think of an idea or know about a question. Are your colleagues in favour of the Company's proposed move? Do they prefer one site to another? Is there anyone working in offices at the new site whose impressions can be sought?

Written sources of information

These range from the reply to the letter you send to the County Surveyor enquiring about the new factory development, to a search through back copies of the local newspaper to see what happened last time a Company the size of yours moved its operations and work force, to the use of reference books of various kinds.

Whichever methods you decide you need to employ to gather the information for your report, you will need to exercise care and skill in note taking. Indicate in your notes where you are quoting the actual words used by your respondent either in speech or in writing. Show also where you are departing from recording a respondent's ideas to interject some thought or comment of your own. Try not to use too many abbreviations which you might forget the meaning of, and when taking notes from written sources, make sure that you have included adequate reference data, for example: 'Mr Manchester's Diary', *Manchester Evening News,* 11 October 1980.

Whatever kind of work you are involved in, it is helpful to keep in your office some of the most commonly-used sources of reference, including telephone directories, post-code and dialling-code directories, a dictionary, road maps or a gazetteer, and a ready-reckoner.

Reports in letter form

There are numerous occasions on which letters are received requesting information which in effect amounts to, and is presented best in the form of, a short report. You may be familiar with this type of report: if you have ever been involved in trying to buy a house, you certainly will be.

As an example, consider the following letter, sent from a firm of Timber Consultants to an Estate Agent:

WESTINGHOUSE & COMPANY LIMITED

Salisbury House
Dorset Street
London EC4 OHB

Our Ref: 78.108/ST/TP
Your Ref: 862/B/ST
22nd March, 1980.

G. Williams Esq.,
Estate Agent,
2A Hastings Road,
LONDON.
SW13P 8WW

Dear Mr Williams,

Contract No. 862, 15 Melling Street

In accordance with your instructions to inspect the above property, an inspection was carried out by our Mr J. Peters on 21st March. Set out below are his observations and recommendations regarding rising damp and other apparent causes of dampness.

Observations

The property inspected was a mid-terraced house constructed in brickwork with 225 mm thick external walls and 112 mm internal walls. The floors were of suspended timber with the exception of the entrance porch and kitchen which were of solid construction. There is an existing poured bitumastic damp proof course throughout the property but this is bridged by the solid floors.
Visual indications of rising damp were marked stains, perished plaster and spoilt decorations and instrumental readings taken at the time of the inspection confirmed the presence of rising damp.

Recommendations

1) Damp Proof Course. We recommend the injection of a Chemical Damp Proof Course, in accordance with our specification, to the walls marked in red on the sketch plan.
Injection will be carried out at inner floor level from inside and outside the property on the walls to be damp proofed.
Our estimates for this work, covered by our 20 year guarantee, are attached.

2) Replastering. It is imperative that replastering be carried out according to our Plastering Specification, a copy of which is printed inside our folder. The following areas should be removed: up to a height of 600 mm from floor level on the walls to be damp proofed. Your own contractor should be instructed to carry out this work. Alternatively, we have included for the removal and renewal of plaster in estimate 'B'.

Condensation.

There was no evidence of condensation at the time of the inspection, but should this problem become apparent, you should contact us for further advice.

Skirtings.

Skirting boards removed by our Technicians to inject the damp proof course will be left on site for refixing by your builder. Alternatively, we have included the renewal of all skirting boards using 19 x 75 bulnose section timbers in our estimate 'B'.

Should you require us to carry out the above work, would you please return the duplicate copy of the appropriate estimate, duly signed, and arrangements will be made to carry out the work.

If you have any queries that you would like to discuss, please do not hesitate to contact us.

Yours sincerely,

S. Tobias
Manager

What we learn from a study of the above 'report-letter' or 'letter-report' is that it is possible to present a report *within* a letter. We begin the letter in the normal way, by saluting the recipient and introducing the material in an opening paragraph, and then proceed to set out methodically our observations and recommendations, employing appropriate headings and numbering the items if this seems to be necessary. When we reach the end of the information to be presented, we round off the letter in the usual way with a polite concluding paragraph and the complimentary close.

Naturally, the same kind of lay-out can be adopted when the reply is to take the form of a memorandum. The usual memorandum headings stand at the top, and the presentation follows under appropriate headings and numbers.

Exercise 6.2. You receive the following note from a superior at work. Write your reply in the form of a memorandum:

> It is well known that numbers of people in office jobs work in conditions which are unpleasant, uncomfortable and unnecessarily so. Sometimes it is a question of a desk in a wrong corner of a badly-ventilated room; sometimes an essential piece of equipment is not available; sometimes there is noise, intermittent or continuous; sometimes the public have difficulty in finding their way to it. On the other hand, when physical conditions are right staff are happy and work is well done. We are asking members of staff to look critically at their physical surroundings. I want you to write a brief report for me on the effect which the place you work in has on yourself and on your work. Make any recommendations you consider practicable, and do not forget to outline the nature of the work you perform.

A report presented schematically

Not all reports, of course, take the form of letters or memoranda. Nor are all reports eye-witness accounts of events that have taken place. We have also to bear in mind the kind of report which calls for an investigation, like Exercise 6.2 above, but leaves the method of presentation up to the writer.

Let us examine in detail an actual case where a report of this kind was asked for, and see what steps the writer took to fulfil the requirements of the request.

In November 1978 Mrs Hughes was asked by her employers, an advertising agency, to produce a report on the proposal to change the organization of office accommodation from a conventional series of small offices opening off both sides of a long corridor, to an open-plan arrangement.

This provided her with the *Terms of Reference* of her report. But as so often happens, the terms of reference themselves required further definition before Mrs Hughes was ready to begin making her enquiries. Was a move of some sort inevitable? Were new premises already chosen? Were all, or only some of, the firm's employees involved in the proposed changes?

Mrs Hughes asked these questions and received the following answers:

> We are forced into a move by the termination of the lease on our

present premises, which have been compulsorily purchased for redevelopment. We have arranged to occupy a complete floor of a new office building under construction on a site adjacent to the present premises, and it is up to us to decide on the interior structure and arrangement of the floor space. We envisage accommodating all staff in the new open-plan offices, if the proposal is shown to be viable.

Having clarified these issues, Mrs Hughes was ready to proceed to the next stage, the *Method of Investigation,* or *Procedure Employed.* When she came to write up her report, she included under this heading an account of all the ways in which she collected the information required. These included in this particular case a summary of the various kinds of work done by the different departments and sections of the company. Each section was issued with questionnaires which asked for a brief description of the kind of work carried out, and all the individual members were asked for their opinions on the suitability of (*a*) small, closed offices and (*b*) larger, open-plan areas for this work. In addition, Mrs Hughes approached a firm of architects and designers with whom her own Company was associated, and asked them to outline the different kinds of open-plan offices which could be contemplated in the case in question. She then made enquiries of customers of the Agency who themselves worked in open-plan situations, in order to arrive at a general assessment of the feasibility of such working conditions.

All the information collected by these various means provided Mrs Hughes with her *Observations,* or *Findings.* Having collected the data required, she was then faced with the task of arranging it in logical order for presentation in her report. To help in this, she adopted a system of numbering, and of headings and sub-headings, as shown in the following specimen page. Note that headings of equal importance are given the same visual impact by the use of capital letters, underlining, etc. In this specimen page the actual findings are omitted, except for the first line in each case.

ANALYSIS OF EMPLOYEES' QUESTIONNAIRES

A. DESCRIPTION OF THE DEPARTMENT'S WORK

Each Department was issued with questionnaires which were

B. MAKING THE OPEN-PLAN SYSTEM WORK

Employees were asked what special provision, if any, they

C. A CLOSER LOOK AT SOME OF THE PROBLEMS

The Production Team

The main worry brought to light here was that customers

```
The Design Team
The same problem of noise was mentioned here, particularly

The Support Team
(a)  Typists
     The only problem mentioned by the typists was the

(b)  Reception
     Both receptionists felt that it would be preferable
```

After the presentation of the findings, a report must reach certain *Conclusions.* Mrs Hughes's report concluded that a change-over to the new style of office contemplated certainly offered advantages, the main one being a great saving of space, but that these advantages were balanced by a number of disadvantages including loss of privacy for clients and increased noise level. In other words, the conclusions are a summing-up and evaluating of the data collected.

If the terms of reference ask for *Recommendations,* these are presented after the conclusions. In the case we have been considering as an example, Mrs Hughes recommended that a limited scale open-plan office should be introduced for the design and secretarial staff, but that separate accommodation was needed for consultation with clients, for the production staff, and for the reception area.

At the end of the report, the signature of the compiler, and the date, should appear.

So the whole report will take the following form:

Title and terms of reference
Statement of Method
Findings
Conclusions
Recommendations (if any)
Signature and date.

If the report is a long one, the reader can be helped to find his way through it by the provision of a *Table of Contents* and possibly even a prefatory summary of the main findings and conclusions.

If the report requires the reader to study tables of statistics or lengthy extracts from official documents, it may be more convenient to present these as *Appendices* at the end, to avoid breaking the continuity of the main body of the report.

Here, then, is the title page of Mrs Hughes's report, with the Table of Contents clearly set out:

OPEN PLAN OFFICES FOR GREAVES ADVERTISING

Report of an Investigation called for by the Directors
November 1978

A note on style in report writing

When a report is to be presented in this formal, or schematic, way, it is best to avoid personal constructions such as 'I asked the fifteen students what they thought', and to use the impersonal 'Fifteen students were asked for their views'. This seems much more business-like and adds authority to your findings.

Exercise 6.3. The idea has been put forward that the college you attend should run a revision course for day-release students just before their examinations. So far, no definite proposals have been made regarding duration, place, dates, and course content. You are asked to submit a report outlining the advantages and possible disadvantages of such a course from the point of view of (*a*) the students, (*b*) the college and (*c*) the employers.

Exercise 6.4. There is a threat of power-cuts this coming winter, and the Director of Social Services in your town is worried about how his Department is going to cope with the crisis such cuts would cause in old people's homes. He asks you to write a report setting out what you think the needs of old people are in such an emergency, and giving your ideas on how these needs can be met. You must, of course, be realistic financially.

Writing up a report from somebody else's notes

Not all reports that people in business and public administration are called upon to write are solely the work of one person. Very often people who work in offices are called upon to write a report from material supplied by someone else. For example, the report on page 53 which was sent by Westinghouse and Company to Mr Williams was probably not presented in the exact form that we saw it when handed in by Mr Peters, the surveyor. What is much more likely is that Mr Peters handed his notes on the condition of the property to a secretary or clerk at the office, who set out his observations and recommendations in an acceptable and easily readable form.

What is required to do such a job is the ability to expand your own or someone else's rough notes and set out information in a logical order, and organise the material to make it look business-like and help the reader find his or her way through it.

Exercise 6.5. Imagine that you work in the Housing Department of your local authority. The authority has been thinking of building a new estate outside the town itself, but there has been a lot of controversy lately in the local press about life and conditions on a similar estate which was built about four years ago. Because of this, a team of sociology students from the local technical college were employed to visit the estate and ask questions. One of them has handed in the notes reproduced below, and you are asked to write these up and present the information in the form of a report to be considered by the Housing Committee. You are asked *not* to make any recommendations.

Notes

Long wait for bus in town centre. Over one hour on bus (not in rush hour).
Local rail station closed down 2 years ago. 60p fare. At the other end told no buses to other outlying estates on periphery of city—only straight into centre—all take same route.
Bus stop on edge of estate—long walk for some.
Mud everywhere. Eviction taking place—crowd of women—I asked them why—said it is always happening: high rent. Much petty crime.
'He had a bag with the *gas meter* in it!'
Women say shops good (but there did not seem to be much choice).
Litter bins full—lots of mess round chip shop—'the road man empties the litter in the stream' (old lady).

> The stream: lots of rubbish. No railings round. Danger for children.
> 'The children get on the garage roofs and throw mud at the windows.'
> 'They broke my gnome's head off.' 'I'm frightened to go out at night.'
> 'They keep that dog chained up howling.' 'Every phone box is broken.'
> 'They even ripped the backs off the benches.' 'If you tell the police they don't do anything.' 'No-one to turn to.'
> Two types of houses—'gas' and 'electric'. Very similar design.
> All the same size. Rent £16 per fortnight (likely to go up soon).
> v. small rooms. 3 beds.
> *Youth*—'We've nothing to do—nowhere to go.' 'The picture house is bingo now.' 'Miles to school'. 'No friends'. 'Nowhere to start a youth club.' 'No football pitches.' 'If you haven't got a car you're stuck.' (Last bus from town 10 p.m.)
> *Age*—'I had a lovely little house, a little palace, and they pulled it down.' 'He doesn't get home till it's nearly time to go to bed.' 'Bus fare £6 a week.' 'I chose to come here. It's lovely, fresh air, fields, can't understand why some people are always moaning.' 'Might as well be dead.' 'They never asked me where I wanted to live.' 'Can't afford to use the central heating.' 'You've got to be a mountain goat to live here.' 'Haven't seen my grandchildren for two years.'

Presenting statistics in a report

Very often, the terms of reference of a report will require the provision of statistical information, and when we are compiling the report, it is necessary for us to consider the best way of presenting such statistics. We must try to be aware of the person or persons to whom we are writing, selecting words carefully, and considering the vocabulary we can take for granted in our readers. When dealing with statistics we have to remember that many highly literate people are what is called 'innumerate', that is to say, they are inept at handling figures. Add to these people those who have difficulty with words *and* numbers, and you will see at once how important it is to present statistics as clearly and simply as possible. A graph, chart or table can show a great deal of information at a glance. Material presented in an eye-catching layout is often remembered more easily than material presented in words alone, and such a visual aid helps to break up the monotony of the report and keep the reader's interest alive. The choice of form of visual aid depends on its purpose. *Tables* are the simplest and can be very effective, as shown by the following example. Consider this information, extracted from a report on slum clearance:

> There are exactly one hundred properties in the road and exactly half are tenanted. The owner-occupiers fall into two categories: the old and the young, representing 25 per cent and 15 per cent of the total occupants, respectively. Although there are only ten shopkeepers, they will, I am sure, demand something like £20 000 each in compensation for their properties and good will. The young people, who have put in new bathrooms with sliding doors etc.—just the sort of thing that pushes up the compensation—are talking in terms of £8 000 per house, a realistic figure in my view. I suppose the poorer properties—the tenanted and the old people's—will merit about £5 000 per property.

Now the information we want to show here is how much it is going to cost if the Council compulsorily purchases all these properties. There are four kinds of owner mentioned: young owner-occupiers (£8 000 each), old owner-occupiers (£5 000 each), landlords of tenanted properties (£5 000 each), and shopkeepers (£20 000 each). We need to show how many of each type there are, and what the total cost will be.

Here is a very simple table which presents the information 'at a glance':

Type of Owner	Number	£ Compensation per property	Total
Young owner-occupiers	15	8000	£120 000
Old owner-occupiers	25	5000	£125 000
Landlords	50	5000	£250 000
Shopkeepers	10	20 000	£200 000
TOTAL			£695 000

Exercise 6.6. Here is a request for a report which calls for the compilation of a table similar to the one above. Read the note, and write the reply requested as a 'schematic' report:

> As you will probably recall, the town carnival last year was linked to the Mayor's appeal fund. The time has come round to prepare for this year's carnival and the new carnival committee has requested a report on last year's efforts estimating the success of each event. I would like you to write this report. The committee is particularly interested in the relative profitability of each event—that is the amount raised per head by each event—and I feel this will be best shown in table form.
>
> The following information on last year's activities has been left on the files by my predecessor:
>
> A buffet lunch in honour of the Carnival Queen's coronation was attended by two hundred people and raised a profit of one hundred pounds; a charity football match—between our local team and a team of local radio personalities—was attended by two thousand people and raised eight hundred and forty pounds; a jumble sale, attended by four hundred people, raised one hundred and thirty-six pounds; donations, collected in tins during the carnival procession, witnessed by approximately four thousand people, raised two hundred and eight pounds; six hundred people bought raffle tickets and the sum of sixty pounds was raised; a dance, attended by three hundred and eighty people, raised one hundred and ninety pounds; sixty people attended a film festival which raised forty pounds.
>
> I should be grateful if, along with your account of last year's events, you would include suggestions on any items which you feel might sensibly be excluded from this year's programme, or indeed any ideas you might have for new events.

Tables are one of the best ways of showing figures both quickly and accurately, but other visual aids come into their own in showing significance and trends, or making comparisons. *Charts* and *graphs* are very effective for these purposes.

When Mrs Hughes asked the staff of Greaves Advertising whether they were in favour of the change-over to open-plan offices, she could have presented her findings in a bar graph, as follows:

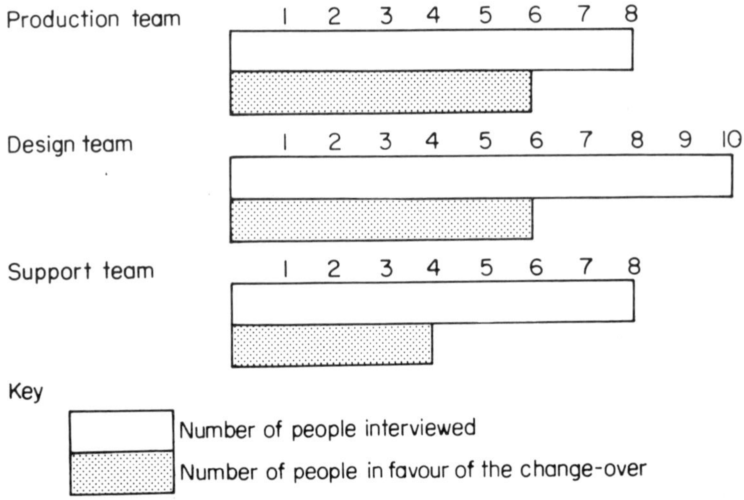

Or she could have shown the difference in response from employees who had experience of working in open-plan offices and those who had not, in a pie chart, as follows:

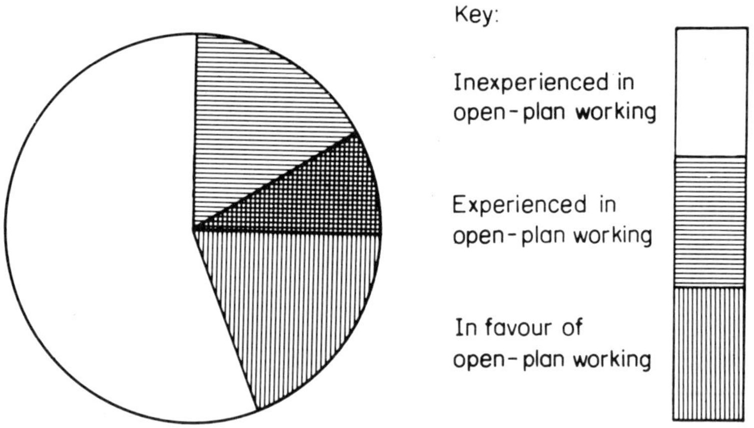

This method of presentation shows clearly the great difference in the proportion of 'inexperienced' and 'experienced' people who were in favour of the change-over. Findings of this kind have great significance in influencing decision-making.

Trends are best indicated by the use of simple graphs. For example, the purchases and sales of a company over a period of weeks or months can be shown in this way:

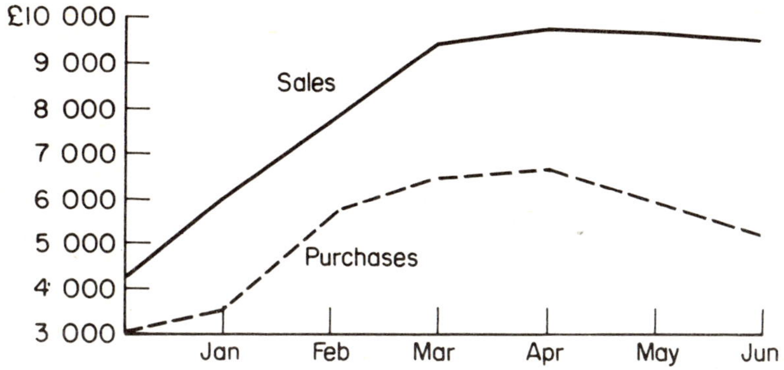

Exercise 6.7: Working in pairs. Turn to Exercise 2.8 on page 23, and write your response in note form. Then exchange notes with your partner and write a brief report from his or her notes. Try to include some statistics of real or imaginary people whose opinions you have sought, and present them in the most effective form.

Exercise 6.8. Your Managing Director is looking for ways in which the Company's offices can be made more efficient. Write a report, outlining the measures which you think would be a help in this respect.

Exercise 6.9. Use whatever methods you consider suitable to find out what the following sets of initials stand for, and write a paragraph on each:

CID	COD	E&OE	HMSO	EEC
JP	NALGO	NATO	TUC	UN

7

Meetings

One of the duties which may fall to your lot at some time is that of acting as Secretary to a Committee. This involves sending out *Notices of meetings* and *Agendas* in time to let the people who are entitled to attend the meeting know when and where it is going to be held and—briefly—what business is going to be conducted. During the meeting itself the Secretary is expected to take notes and from these to produce a concise and orderly record of who attended and what decisions were taken. This record is called the *Minutes* of the meeting, and there are certain conventions about the lay out of such minutes, and also about the order of the items on the agenda.

The notice of a meeting

This is simply to inform people of the date, time and venue of the meeting, and because it will be accompanied or followed-up by an agenda, there is no need to state the business. Very often it will take the form of a letter, such as the following:

Westchester Committee For Mental Health

Secretary: *G.H Timmons,*
18 Wellesby Street,
Green Park,
Westchester.
WE7 30H.

17 March 1980

Dear

<u>March Meeting of the Committee</u>

The next monthly meeting of the Committee has been arranged for 31 March to accommodate Dr Evans. It will take place at 6.00 p.m. in Committee Room B, Westchester Central Library.

An agenda for this meeting is enclosed, and I hope that you will be able to attend.

Yours sincerely,

GEORGE TIMMONS
Secretary

The agenda for a meeting

This is a list of the business which will be conducted, and there is a special order in which to present the items. *Apologies for absence* are usually taken first, and these are followed by a reading of the *Minutes of the last meeting,* which are then agreed as a correct record and signed by the Chairman (or the meeting may agree to 'take the minutes as read' if they have been circulated well in advance.) Then *Matters arising* from these minutes are dealt with. These are followed by the *Secretary's Report,* which usually includes an account of correspondence received, replies sent, and other action taken. Then come the other items of business, which will obviously vary according to the purpose of the meeting, and the last two items on the agenda will be *Any Other Business,* where members of the committee can raise issues which have come to their attention since the agenda was compiled, and the *date and time of the next meeting.*

A specimen agenda for the above (imaginary) meeting would look like this:

AGENDA

1. Apologies for absence
2. Minutes of the meeting held on 28th February 1980
3. Matters arising
4. Secretary's Report
5. Report by Dr Evans on the Blackpool Conference
6. Purchase of a minibus
7. Summer holiday arrangements
8. Any other business
9. Date of next meeting

Combined notice and agenda

It is possible to combine the notice of a meeting and the agenda and present them on one sheet of paper. This is obviously very economical and you may well be wondering why it is not always done in this way. The main reason is that it is often not possible to prepare an agenda a long time in advance, whereas it is obviously important to give people plenty of notice that a meeting is going to take place, so that they will keep the time free to attend.

However, if the agenda *is* decided well in advance, then there are two alternative ways in which the combined notice/agenda can be set out. The first way is to incorporate the agenda into the letter giving notice of the meeting, thus:

Westchester Committee For Mental Health

Secretary: *G.H Timmons,*
18 Wellesby Street,
Green Park,
Westchester.
WE7 30H.

17 March 1980

Dear

Notice of Meeting

The next monthly meeting of the Committee has been arranged for 31 March, to accommodate Dr Evans. It will take place at 6.00 p.m. in Committee Room B, Westchester Central Library.

The Agenda for the meeting will be as follows:

1. Apologies for absence
2. Minutes of the meeting held on 28 February 1980
3. Matters arising
4. Secretary's Report
5. Report by Dr Evans on the Blackpool Conference
6. Purchase of a Minibus

7. Summer Holiday arrangements
8. Any other business
9. Date of next meeting

I hope that you will be able to attend.

Yours sincerely,

GEORGE TIMMONS
Secretary

If the notice and agenda are not to be sent out in the form of a letter, through the post, but can simply be handed to people working in the same organisation, or put up on a notice-board, they may be set out like this:

WESTCHESTER TRANSPORT DEPARTMENT

STAFF SPORTS AND SOCIAL CLUB

The Annual General Meeting of the Club will be held on 31st March 1980 at 12.15 p.m. in the canteen. All members are urged to attend.

ORDER OF BUSINESS

1. Apologies for absence
2. Minutes of the Annual General Meeting held on 29th March 1979
3. Matters arising
4. Secretary's Report
5. Treasurer's Report
6. Election of Officers for 1980-1
    A. Chairman
    B. Secretary
    C. Treasurer
7. Any other business
8. Date of next A.G.M.

STEPHEN WORSLEY

Secretary

You will note from the above that an Annual General Meeting includes a Treasurer's Report so that members can be informed of their financial position. Instead of the word 'Agenda', 'Order of Business' has been used, which is quite an acceptable alternative.

Exercise 7.1. Prepare a Notice of Meeting and an Agenda for an ordinary meeting (*not* an A.G.M.) of *either* your local Eighteen-Plus Group *or* a college club or society. You may present this in any format which you consider suitable.

Minutes of a meeting

The keeping of good and useful minutes is an art. It calls for the exercise of a number of skills.

Minutes should be grammatical. They should be written in complete sentences, so that they make complete sense. This is most important since Committee members are required to agree that the minutes are a 'true record' of what took place at the meeting, and they can hardly be expected to do that if they cannot understand them.
Minutes are an accurate record and require careful judgment in taking notes.
Minutes are a concise record. To compile them the Secretary will need to be able to *summarise* discussion and correspondence.
Minutes should be correctly displayed and numbered and should employ headings and sub-headings to guide the reader through the material. In this, they resemble reports, but they are much more summary than a report.

As in the case of the Agenda, there is a certain order laid down for the presentation of the items. The usual order is as follows:

1. A heading including details of the type of meeting (Committee Meeting, Annual General Meeting, etc.), the location and the time.
2. A list of those attending the meeting, beginning with the name of the Chairman and ending with the names of the Secretary and any other officers.
3. Apologies for absence.
4. Minutes of the last meeting.
5. Matters arising.
6. Secretary's Report or Correspondence.
7. Other items on the Agenda in the order in which they arose. All resolutions should be recorded in the exact words used when moved.
8. Any other business—again dealt with in the order in which items were raised.
9. Date of the next meeting.
10. Space for the Chairman's signature, and the date of the meeting.

Making notes for minutes

Even if it were possible to record verbatim (word for word) everything which was said at a meeting, it would in most cases be neither necessary nor desirable. The important parts of the meeting, which must be noted in the minutes, are those which will affect future action and decisions. In order to make this possible, the order of business should be followed carefully. You will have the Agenda in advance, and can note down the items one by one, as headings ready to receive your notes on resolutions and decisions as they are taken.

The following example gives an idea of how much you would be required to write on each of the items on the agenda given above for the meeting of the Westchester Committee for Mental Health. First read the verbatim report of the discussion on the first four items, and then study the minutes which follow.

Verbatim report

Mr Garrett Well, here we are. Is everybody here? No—apologies? Have we got some apologies?—Right, thank you George. It's after six now, ladies and gentlemen, if you don't mind—I'd like to call the meeting to order now. Order, please! Thank you. Well, ladies and gentlemen, welcome to this monthly meeting of the Westchester Committee for Mental Health. Everybody seems to be here except Mrs Bennett, Mr Cross and Mr Cordell, and we've received apologies for absence from them. So shall we proceed to the Minutes of the last meeting? Do we need to read them ? Everybody's had a chance to read them, I think? Shall we take them as read?

Various Members Yes, Aye, etc.

Mr Garrett Will somebody please move the Minutes as a correct record?

Mr Jones So move.

Mr Garrett Seconder?

Mr Balian Second.

Mr Garrett Thank you. The Minutes are accepted as a true record. I'll sign them, thank you. Matters arising? Any matters arising? Miss Hague?

Miss Hague I'd like to ask the Secretary through you, Mr Chairman, if we have had any reply yet to the letter we sent to the Rotary Club asking for money.

Mr Garrett George?

Mr Timmons No, Mr Chairman. We've heard nothing.

Miss Hague Then may I suggest, Mr Chairman, that we ask Mr Timmons to write again to see if we can get anything from them?

Mr Garrett It is suggested by Miss Hague that we should ask the Secretary to write again to the Rotary Club, requesting financial assistance. What is the feeling of the meeting?

Various Members Aye, yes, etc.

Mr Garrett Very well, the meeting feels that we should write again. George, will you do that, please?

Mr Timmons Right.

Mr Garrett Any further matters? Yes, Mr Dunne?

Mr Dunne Just like to report, Mr Chairman, that my letter to the Poly hasn't come up with anything yet.

Mr Garrett That was your letter regarding local research programmes into mental handicap, wasn't it?

Mr Dunne Aye. 'Course, it's early days yet, but I thought I'd best let you know.

Mr Garrett Yes, thank you Mr Dunne. No doubt you will keep us informed of any future developments. George, did you want to say something?

Mr Timmons Yes. You'll remember I wrote to Dr Carney of the General Hospital to ask him if he'd like to address our next meeting. Well, this is his reply here, and he says he'd be very pleased to come if we can agree on a suitable date towards the end of April.

Mr Garrett Thank you. Any further matters? No? Right. Perhaps the Secretary would like to present his report?

Mr Timmons Yes. Thank you, Mr Chairman. Well, no doubt you'll all be very pleased to hear that I won't keep you very long, tonight, for a change. Just a few odds and ends. I've received a letter from a lady in Haverton, a Mrs McGhee. She's asking about compensation for vaccine-damaged children. I haven't taken any action on this one yet, as I only got the letter on Monday, but I think it's a little bit out of our scope really. What I'd like to suggest, if everybody's agreeable, is that we should send her one of those booklets that Mr Purvis gave us when he came to address the meeting in January.

Mrs Cotterrel Yes, and perhaps, Mr Chairman, we could put this lady in touch with Mr Purvis. It's obvious that he's the person she really needs.

Mr Garrett Everyone agreed? All right, then, Mr Secretary, send this lady the National Society's Booklet, and put her in touch with Mr Purvis.

Mr Timmons Right-oh, Mr Chairman. Now, I have here the latest issue of the National Society's Bulletin. It runs to twelve pages, Mr Chairman. I've read it all, and it's all good stuff, but I'm sure you don't all want to be stuck here till midnight while I read it out to you. On the other hand, it's a bit too much for me to make an abstract of. So I thought the Committee might like to agree to having it photocopied so that everyone can have their own copy.

Mr Garrett Sounds like a good idea to me, George. What does everyone else think?

Miss Hague Good idea, it's always well worth reading.

Mr Dunne Aye, let's have it photocopied.

Mr Garrett Right, that's settled then. The Secretary to arrange for photocopying.

Mr Timmons Well, that's it, then, Mr Chairman, except to tell you I've written to Davies and Whitelow, like you asked me to last month, to see if their 'Care' group would like to give us a hand to keep the minibus on the road, now that we've got it.

Minutes

WESTCHESTER COMMITTEE FOR MENTAL HEALTH

Minutes of a meeting held at 6.00 p.m. on 31st March 1980 in Committee Room B, Westchester Central Library

Present: Mr S. Garrett (in the chair)
Mrs P. Cotterrel, Miss M. Hague,
Messrs J. Dunne, M. Jones, O. Balian,
Dr D. Evans.
Mr G. Timmons (Secretary)

1. Apologies for Absence were received from Ms G. Bennett and Messrs D. Cross and J. Cordell.

2. Minutes of the Meeting of 28th February 1980 were agreed as a true record and signed by the Chairman.

3. Matters Arising

3.1. Miss Hague asked if any response had been forthcoming from the Rotary Club following the Committee's application for assistance. The Secretary reported that it had not and was asked to make a further application.

3.2. Mr Dunne reported that his enquiries at the Polytechnic had not so far uncovered any information about research being carried out locally.

3.3. The Secretary reported that Dr S.J. Carney of Trimfield General Hospital had accepted the invitation to speak at the next meeting of the Committee.

4. Secretary's Report

4.1. A letter had been received from Mrs McGhee of Haverton, requesting information about compensation for vaccine-damaged children. The Secretary was requested to send her the National Society's booklet and the address of Mr Purvis.

4.2. The latest bulletin of the National Society had been received, and it was agreed that the Secretary should arrange for photocopying so that every member could have a copy.

4.3. A letter had been sent to Davies & Whitelow Ltd asking if their "Care" group would be interested in helping to maintain the new minibus.

5. Report on the Blackpool Conference

Dr Evans presented a comprehensive report on the Conference held in Blackpool in January, which he attended on behalf of the Committee. A copy of this report will be available to each member at the next meeting. The Chairman thanked Dr Evans for his efforts on the Committee's behalf.

6. Purchase of a Minibus

Miss Hague reported that the Minibus which had been offered by the Education Committee had been purchased for £1,200. This left the Committee owing the bank £400. Mrs Cotterrel suggested that fund-raising should be put on the agenda for the next meeting, and this was agreed.

7. Summer Holiday Arrangements

No progress had so far been made, and it was agreed that this item should be put on the agenda for the April meeting.

8. Any Other Business

The Chairman reported that the Westchester Chronicle had recently carried an article about the proposed closure of the Handicapped Youth Centre in Dinton as part of the cuts in public spending. It was resolved that 'a letter should be sent to the Chronicle

```
    protesting about this proposal' and the Secretary was
    asked to write as soon as possible.

9.  Date of Next Meeting

    It was agreed that the next meeting should be held
    on the latest date in April acceptable to Dr Carney.

The meeting closed at 8.25 p.m.

                              ......................

                              Chairman
```

Exercise 7.2. Write the minutes of the meeting for which you prepared the notice and agenda in Exercise 7.1.

Exercise 7.3. Compose a notice of meeting and an agenda for the Annual General Meeting of the local branch of the trade union or students' union to which you belong.

Exercise 7.4. Write the minutes of the meeting referred to in Exercise 7.3.

Exercise 7.5. Turn to Exercise 2.2 on page 17, and write the minutes of the meeting referred to in examples (*a*) and (*b*).

Exercise 7.6: Group assignment

(*a*) Elect a member of your class to act as Chairman.
(*b*) Draft an agenda for a meeting of the students on your course, called to discuss whether any alterations should be made to the syllabus before the next intake of students arrives.
(*c*) Using a tape-recorder to record your discussion, hold the meeting.
(*d*) Write the minutes of the meeting.

Exercise 7.7. Read the following passage carefully and then write a brief definition of the words in italics. Use whatever reference books you need to obtain the information.

> At an *ad hoc* meeting of the Public Relations *Sub-Committee* held on Tuesday 1 March, under *Standing Order* III (iv), it was *resolved* not to *co-opt* the Managing Director's secretary. The *motion* was *proposed* by Mr Davies, who explained that since the meetings often failed to achieve a *quorum*, an extra member would be beneficial. Mr Levy attempted to move an *amendment* but did not find a *seconder*. A proposal that the suggestion should *lie on the table* also received no support. When Mrs Carter asked that the *question be put*, the *Chairman* had to use his *casting vote*, and explained that as it was customary to do so in favour of the *status quo*, he would have to defeat the motion. A motion to *refer back* the question of advertising expenditure to the *Treasurer* was passed *nem con*.

8

Other Forms of Communication

Designing a form

Have you ever experienced difficulty in filling in a form? I have, and I have had many complaints from the students I teach about the forms that they have to fill in to enrol at college or to enter for their examinations. When we look into the causes of these complaints, they seem to fall into a number of categories:

Insufficient information provided on how to fill in the form;
Badly worded or punctuated questions;
Insufficient space left for the information requested;
No indication where the form should be sent after it has been completed.

As with every other kind of communication, it is possible to work out a simple strategy which will make sure that such mistakes do not occur on the forms that we design.

First of all, we must work out what we are going to say at the top of the first page. It is a good idea to supply a heading, similar to the sort we put at the top of a letter. If we use as our example a simple application form of the type used when applying for a job, we can start off by putting:

WESTCHESTER COUNTY COUNCIL

Application for the post of ....

Then, if we require a preamble to explain the purpose of the form, that can come next. A simple preamble suitable for our example would be:

Please answer *all* questions in your own handwriting.
If you do not know the answer to a question, please write 'd.k.' in the space provided. Do not leave any blank spaces.

Next, we have to consider what information we need to obtain. In the case of this form, a prospective employer will want to know the full names, address and age of the applicant, details of his or her secondary school and college education; what examinations he or she has passed and any examination results which are still awaited; particulars of previous employment, including the names and addresses of employers, the nature of their business, the capacity in which the applicant was employed, the work he or she actually did, and how much salary was received for it. In addition, it is usual to enquire about the reasons for leaving at least the present employment and applying for the new post. Finally, the employer needs to know when the applicant could commence in the new post and from whom references can be obtained.

Having decided what we want to know, we have to decide in what order we want the information presented, how we are going to word and punctuate the questions and how much space we need to leave for each item.

Order. It obviously makes sense to ask for personal details first and then elicit the more specialised information.

Wording. It is surprising how many forms one comes across which ask the respondent to fill in his 'Christian names'. This overlooks the fact that a very large number of English-speaking people are Jews, Muslims, or members of other religions, or indeed of no religion at all. It is plainly discourteous to word a question in this way, especially as there are the alternatives 'First names' or 'Forenames' which cannot possibly give offence to anyone.

Punctuation. This should be consistent. If you are going to use questions, then questions should be used throughout, and they should have question marks at the ends. Otherwise, headings may be used. The two alternatives are:

Questions, e.g. What is your full name? How old are you?

Headings, e.g. Name Age

Space. It seems obvious that almost everybody's address is longer than his or her name, and yet many forms leave insufficient space. The same applies in the case of educational qualifications and details of previous employment. If you want full information, you must provide the respondent with sufficient space to give it to you.

Finally, unbelievable as it may seem, I have seen more than one form which failed to indicate where it was to be sent after completion. You should give a full address, with the postcode and, if applicable, indicate an individual to whom it should be directed. Another piece of useful information is the date by which the completed form should reach its destination. These details may be given either at the top of the first page or at the bottom of the last page

If your form is a more complicated one than the example we have just been considering, you may need to provide one or two explanatory notes. These should be kept to a minimum and should be worded extremely simply. Again, they may appear at the top of the form or as numbered footnotes. Ideally, however, your questions should be so explicit that such notes will not be necessary.

Completing a form

If you are on the receiving end of the form, instead of having to design it, the task is even simpler. But you should make sure that you read the instructions fully before attempting to complete the form. Always fill in the whole form. If some sections or questions do not apply to you, write 'not applicable' in the space provided. This will remove any doubts as to why you have not provided the information requested.

Exercise 8.1. Your employer is finding some difficulty in reconciling the needs for cuts in expenditure with fulfilling the requirements of the Chronically Sick and Disabled Persons Act 1970. In order to try to ascertain that any cuts made do not contravene the provisions of the Act, it has been decided that a register of disabled employees will have to be compiled. For this purpose, you have been asked to draft a form to be distributed to all handicapped employees who work in your building.

The information required will be the name of the person, the Department he or she works in, the nature of the actual work, the hours worked, the nature of the disability, special provisions needed to cope with the handicap, whether such provisions are made and if so, by whom, and any provisions which the respondent feels are needed but are not made.

The form should explain the purpose of the enquiry and should provide a space for any additional information the respondent may wish to give.

Exercise 8.2. Turn to Exercise 2.1 on page 14 and design application forms suitable for use in the cases of examples (*a*), (*b*) and (*c*).

Exercise 8.3. Design a form to be filled in by students wishing to take the course which you are at present following.

All your forms should be exchanged for those designed by other members of the class, and filled in. Completing each other's forms is the best way of detecting deficiencies in design.

Drafting a notice

A notice will not be noticed unless it is noticeable. It is not sent to an individual in an envelope which he or she has to open to see what is inside. It is intended to be posted up on a notice-board and it stands a very good chance of being read by nobody at all.

Drafting an attention-getting notice is an exercise in composition, in conciseness and in display.

Composition

As with all other forms of communication, it is necessary to decide in advance exactly what we want to say, and in what order we want to say it. If the notice is giving information, this should be clearly and simply worded, especially if it is to be read by the general public. If it is giving instructions, these should of course be worded politely, and should be in chronological order, and all the information must be given which people will need in order to carry out the instructions.

Conciseness

Once we know what we want to say, we have to think how we can say it in as few words as possible. The point to remember here is to give *only* as much information as is necessary. If you want people to attend an important meeting, obviously you have to tell them where it is to be held, but it is not your job to provide a road-map as part of the notice.

Display

Nobody wants to stand in front of a notice-board reading a closely-covered page of small print. Too many notices look more like essays. To avoid this it is best to set out the information or instructions in single sentences, one to a line, with spaces between the lines. Not only does this make it easier to read, it also helps to imprint it on people's minds.

Exercise 8.4. Turn back to Exercise 2.11, page 24, and instead of composing a memorandum, put the instructions into a notice to go up in each office in the building, showing how you think it should be set out.

Exercise 8.5. Turn to Exercise 2.9 on page 24 and using the information given there, draft a notice to be displayed in Southdown College of Further Education.

Exercise 8.6. The bank where you work has been damaged by fire and will be closed for several weeks. In consequence, customers' accounts have been transferred to four other branches in the north, south, east and west areas of the town, but all customers will be able to make deposits and withdrawals (up to £50) at any of these branches, on production of proof of identity. You are asked to:

(*a*) Compose a circular letter to all customers, explaining the position and the arrangements that have been made; and
(*b*) Draft a notice to be displayed in the window of the damaged premises for the benefit of any customers arriving before they receive the letter.

Exercise 8.7. Turn to Exercise 2.2 on page 17 and draft a notice of the fund-raising event referred to in example (*c*).

Persuasive writing: leaflets and advertisements

The drafting of leaflets and advertisements is an exercise in the art of displaying material to its best advantage.

Our very first concern is to use the right words, and when we wish to persuade people to do something, or go somewhere, we need to choose words which both mean exactly what we want them to mean and are easily understood by all sections of the community.

Then we must think about giving instructions, making them accurate, concise and easy to follow. This is very important in this kind of communication, where we may well be telling people to go somewhere or do something.

Our third concern is to write in sentences so that what we have to say will make complete sense, and to punctuate it correctly, and we follow this by a consideration of the kind of 'tone' that should be employed. This is obviously of prime importance when we want not only to persuade people to do what we want them to do, but also, as far as possible, to convince them that they like it.

Conciseness also comes into this exercise, because we will have only a limited amount of space to fill and our readers will have only a limited amount of attention and interest to bestow on what we have written.

The way in which we display the information or instructions will have a considerable effect on the response we are likely to get.

In the exercises which follow, you will have to be very tactful and diplomatic, as you will readily appreciate that you are dealing here with the kind of issues which can generate unrest and resentment if handled thoughtlessly.

Exercise 8.8. Design a leaflet about a change-over to a new system of refuse collection in a trial area of the city. (Instead of the old-style dustbins which have to be picked up and carried to the collection vehicle, emptied and taken back to where they belong, the new system employs paper sacks which only involve the operative in one journey. The sacks fit into lidded steel mesh containers attached to concrete posts. The dustman will leave a clean sack inside the container each week.)

Exercise 8.9. The Housing Department in which you work has decided to set up a number of sub-offices on large council estates, where tenants will be expected to go in future to pay their rents. When the idea was first mentioned in the press, there was an unfavourable reaction from some members of the public, who wrote to the local newspaper stating that some tenants would resent having to start leaving their homes to pay the rent, and that many pensioners welcomed the rent collector as one of their few visitors. Because of this, the Housing Manager is trying to tread warily now that the scheme is actually going to be introduced. Accordingly, he asks you to:

(*a*) produce a draft of a half-page advertisement to appear in the local newspaper, outlining the scheme and attempting to make it as attractive as possible, and

(*b*) write a circular letter to be sent to all pensioners on the estates, again mentioning the change, but also inviting them to contact the Department if they envisage it causing them any problems.

Exercise 8.10. The Youth Club of which you are a member plans to hold a jumble sale to raise funds. One of the members can get leaflets printed cheaply. Draw up a suitable leaflet to distribute to households in the neighbourhood, asking for support in providing jumble, cash, etc. Remember to supply suitable details to make the exercise credible.

Conclusion: From Classroom to Office

By the time you have worked your way through all the exercises in this book, you should feel confident of your ability to understand what is being communicated to you either in speech or in writing, and of your competence in communicating your own thoughts and feelings both orally and in written form. You should by now be able to follow instructions and to take notes which will still make sense when you come back to them after a time. You should be able to write a letter, a memorandum or a report which will be understood easily by the reader for whom it is intended. You should even be able to draft a notice, a leaflet, or an advertisement which will ensure the results you want. In addition, you will have the ability to express your opinions and display your knowledge in the form of an essay for examination purposes.

However, no textbook can teach you everything you need to know and to be able to do in order to function efficiently in a business or public administration post. There is much you will have to learn in your place of work itself. We touched briefly on the question of house style in Chapter 2, but offices differ in many more ways that those in which correspondence is displayed and signed. The particular practices of your own office or organisation will have to be learned as you become familiar with your work.

There are a number of ways in which you can help yourself in this respect. Do not expect to remember everything you are told unless you keep a notebook in which you can write down various points of office or business practice as they occur. Make a point of building up a library of reference books which will make life easier for you. These should include: a good dictionary; telephone directories, including the dialling code booklet; an A-Z or similar guide to your town; an AA or RAC handbook; transport guides to your area and to national routes and services. Other books worth keeping by you are: Roget's *Thesaurus of English Words and Phrases*—particularly useful if your work includes composing letters and other documents, as it provides alternative ways of expressing ideas which help to avoid repetition; an atlas—particularly if your work involves transport or travel; a *Who's Who* or similar guide to personalities; a book such as Burke's *Peerage* which will enable you to avoid errors in etiquette.

The list of books you require will depend on the kind of work you are doing.

In addition, the best source of reference and information is often not a book, but a person. If you cultivate a helpful, interested attitude towards your work, your colleagues will quickly realise the value of spending a little time explaining to you how the work is done. Get into the habit of reading a good newspaper which will keep you informed of the latest developments affecting your work. In fact, soak up all the knowledge you can about your job, and cultivate discretion when you talk about it. Many kinds of work involve contact with private and confidential information about other people's lives, and the ability to forget what you have seen or heard when you leave the office can be as important as the ability to remember it while you are still there.

When you have passed your examination, whether you are already working or still a full-time student, remember that this is only the beginning. Once you start out on your business career, there is no limit to how far you can go, but promotion is something which has to be earned by hard work. I hope that you enjoy it.

Appendix

Parts of speech

'Parts of speech' is an expression used to refer to the different functions that words may perform within a sentence. A sentence is a group of words which makes complete sense, and in order for it to make complete sense a group of words must include a verb.

Verbs

Verbs are words of action, or 'doing' words. They tell us what happens. The simplest verb is the verb 'to be'—I am, you are, he is, etc. But when we identify the verb in a sentence, we have to make sure that the verb itself is complete. For example, the verb 'to run' has a form 'running', but 'running' requires another word with it to make it function as a verb. It needs 'was', 'were', 'am', or 'will be'. These words indicate the *tense* of the verb, whether it is past, present, or future.

Past tense forms	**Present tense forms**	**Future tense forms**
I *had been running*	I *run*	I *will run* or *shall run*
I *have been running*	I *am running*	I *will be running*
I *was running*		I *will have run*
I *ran*		I *will have been running*
		I *am going to run*

The words which stand before the various forms of 'run' are called 'auxiliary' words and they are necessary because unless we know whether the action *has* happened, *is* happening, or *is going to* happen (*will* happen), the sentence will not make complete sense.

Subjects of verbs. Complete sense also requires an indication of who or what is performing the activity referred to by the verb. We want to know *who* is running, or *what* happened. The word in the sentence which gives us this information is called the 'subject'. Subjects can be of two kinds, they can be either nouns, or pronouns.

Nouns

Nouns are naming words, and they can be divided into various kinds.

Common nouns name things and people of which many examples can be found: house, tree, road, picture, book, school, desk, floor, man, clerk, student, baby.

All common nouns have singular and plural forms. Many plural forms are made by adding 's'—houses, trees, roads, pictures, books, schools. Others are subject to certain rules. Nouns where the singular form ends in 'y' take the plural 'ies'—babies, groceries, ladies. Others have irregular forms—men, children, memoranda, cacti. These have to be memorised.

Proper nouns name particular things and people. Florence Little—my name—is a proper noun, or two proper nouns. London, Liverpool, Brisbane, Nigeria and Europe are all proper nouns. So are Tuesday and December. Names of offices held by individuals count as proper nouns, for example, Prime Minister and Chancellor of the Exchequer. A particular road, such as Melling Street, is a name, and therefore a proper noun, and this applies also to government and local authority departments and committees, like the Department of Health and Social Security and the Education Committee.

You will have noticed that proper nouns always begin with capital letters.

Abstract nouns refer to intangible properties, such as beauty, truth, goodness, loyalty, pride, gluttony, sloth, efficiency and punctuality.

Collective nouns are words used to identify groups of common nouns, such as a *flock* of sheep, a *herd* of cattle, a *shoal* of herrings, a *class* of students.

Pronouns

'Pro' means 'for', as in 'pros' and 'cons' which means 'points for and against'. A pronoun is therefore a word which stands in place of a noun. There are only a limited number of pronouns—called personal pronouns—which can do duty as subjects of verbs. They are: I, you, he, she, it, we, you, they.

Examples

Florence Little is going to take a holiday becomes *I am going to take a holiday.*
The reader of this book is nearing the end becomes *You are nearing the end.*
Mr Walker reached for the telephone becomes *He reached for the telephone.*
The door needs reparing becomes *It needs repairing.*

There are other personal pronouns to use when the person referred to is not the subject, but the object, of the verb, that is, when instead of doing something, something is being done to him/her.

Subjective Personal Pronouns	Objective Personal Pronouns
I	me
you	you
he	him
she	her
it	it
we	us
you	you
they	them

Examples

I (subjective) spoke to him (objective).
She (subjective) contacted us (objective).

Unless the personal pronoun is the subject of the verb, always use the objective form. Say 'Angela and *I* came home late last night', but 'Father was waiting up for Angela and *me*'.

Possessive pronouns indicate ownership, and can be used only *in place of* (standing for) nouns. They are: mine, your, his, hers, ours, yours, theirs.

Examples

Whose is that hat? It is *mine.*
Theirs is the end house.

Demonstrative pronouns demonstrate, or point out, particular things or people, and again they *stand for* nouns.

Examples

Take *this* to your Bank Manager and get it signed.
I prefer these shoes to *those.*

Relative pronouns refer to nouns or pronouns used earlier in the sentence, and are used to avoid repetition or clumsy constructions.

Examples

The team, *who* lost the game, were deeply disappointed.
The newspaper, *which* was a good one, unfortunately ceased publication last year.

Adjectives

Adjectives are words which describe nouns. They include simple words like large, small, green, red, yellow, perfect, delicious and ugly. They include also some more specialised words which are often confused with some of the types of pronouns considered above.

Possessive adjectives tell us who owns things, when the nouns naming the things are present in the sentence. They are: my, your, his, her, its, our, your and their.

Examples

It is *my* hat that she is wearing.
Their house burned down last night.

These words are adjectives because they accompany nouns, they do not replace them.

Demonstrative adjectives demonstrate, or point out, particular nouns, which they accompany in the sentence.

Examples

Take *this* declaration to your Bank Manager, and get it signed.
I prefer *these* shoes.

Adverbs

Adverbs are also descriptive, but they describe *how* the action of a verb is performed. They include words like quickly, slowly, sadly, many of which are formed by adding 'ly' to adjectives. It is important to remember to use the correct form.

Example

He is a *powerful* swimmer (adjective); but He swam *powerfully* (adverb).

Prepositions

Prepositions are words which indicate relationships between other words in a sentence.

Examples

Put the book *down.*
On the table?
No, *under* it.

Other prepositions are: in, to, form, at, until, before and after.

Conjunctions

Conjunctions are words which join together single words or groups of words.

Examples

Bread *and* butter
I took the examination *but* I failed.

It is impossible in many cases to look at a word and know simply by its spelling what part of speech it is, since identical words can be used to perform a number of different functions. Examination papers no longer require candidates to analyse sentences and identify parts of speech, but it is useful to know the different functions in order to understand why a sentence is well or badly constructed, rather than having to rely on a vague feeling that it 'sounds right' or 'looks wrong'.

Punctuation marks

The Full Stop (.)

This is used at the end of a sentence, which is a group of words making complete sense.

Initials and Abbreviations. It is usual to punctuate a name such as H. D. Stein by placing a full stop after each of the initials, and certainly this is advisable when, for example, a letter is hand written. However, the use of full stops after abbreviations in typed and printed matter is now almost universally discontinued. This applies to sets of initials in common use, such as JP, BBC, PAYE, or contractions like Mr and Mrs and to abbreviations like eg and etc. This may be found to vary with the 'house styles' of different organisations.

The Question Mark (?)

This is used after a direct question in actual speech, such as: 'Are we going home?' It is also used after an *implied* question, where the form of words is not that of a question, but the intention is to seek a reply, for example, 'We're not going home already?'

A question mark should never be used with an indirect question, a question reported in indirect speech. Use it only when quoting the actual words used by the speaker when the question was asked.

The Exclamation Mark (!)

This is a perfectly respectable punctuation mark which can be very useful in its proper place. Unfortunately it is so often over-used that it tends to lose its effectiveness. It has no place in business communications.

Inverted Commas ('. . .') and (". . .")

Sometimes called quotation marks, these are put round speech to indicate the actual words used by a speaker. They are not needed in indirect or reported speech. They are also used for quotations from books and documents. It does not really matter which form you use, double or single, unless you are likely to be quoting inside a quotation, when the convention now is to use the double marks inside the single.

Example

> The speaker concluded by saying: 'As William Shakespeare has so wisely enjoined us, "Neither a borrower nor a lender be."'

The Comma (,)

This handy little mark has few rules governing its use. It is often used to indicate a pause, and that is certainly one function it can perform. It is commonly used before and after speech, as 'Good gracious', said Auntie, 'Can that really be the time?'

It is used to separate words in lists: I'll go and buy some coffee, tea, sugar and milk. Note that there is no comma before 'and milk' since the other two commas are replacing the word 'and'.

The comma may also be used to separate words or phrases from the main meaning of the sentence, as in the following examples:

> Well, John, where have you been all day?
> Borrowing, according to Shakespeare, is a bad habit to get into.
> The team, who had suffered injuries, lost by five goals to one.

A comma should never be used to join two groups or words which are complete sentences, however short they may be. If you do not wish to separate them by a full stop, join them by using a conjunction such as 'and'.

The Dash (—)

Like the comma, the dash has several uses. A pair of dashes may be used as an alternative to commas or brackets to mark off a parenthesis, as:

> The monkeys—the subject of the programme—were natives of South America.

It may also be used to create suspense, as in:

> He had everything a man could want: a home, a family, a loving wife—and money.

The dash is useful in summarising a list, for example: Camembert, Edam, Double Gloucester, Port Salut—these are all good cheeses.

The Colon (:)

This may be used to introduce a list, as: I have read several books by Charles Dickens: *Oliver Twist, David Copperfield, Bleak House* and *The Old Curiosity Shop.*

It may introduce a quotation, as: In your letter of 8 July, you stated: 'We have no record of having received any payment from you since 21 February.'

Another use of the colon is to divide up a sentence where the second half explains the first. For example: Mr Jones said he was going home: he said he had a headache.

The Semi-colon (;)

This is a useful punctuation mark with which to break up a long sentence, or to use where two sentences are closely connected in thought but no conjunction is employed. For example: George paused with his key in the lock; he listened for a moment with his head on one side; then he slowly withdrew the key and cautiously tiptoed round to the side of the house.

The Apostrophe (')

This is used to indicate the omission of one or more letters. It is important to insert the apostrophe in the correct place. For example,

I do not becomes *I don't*
He did not becomes *he didn't*
We were not becomes *we weren't*
Note: *It will not* becomes *it won't.*

Such usage of the apostrophe in business correspondence is not good practice, however.

The apostrophe is also used to indicate ownership or possession. The rule here is:

When the possessor is singular, add 's. For example: The man's coat, the boy's bat, the student's book.

When the possessor is a plural form which does not end in s, add 's. For example, The men's coats, the women's hats, the children's games.

When the plural possessor ends in s, an apostrophe only (without the s) is added. For example: the boys' bats, the students' books, the ladies' hats.

Note that *it's* is an abbreviated form of *it is. Its* (possessive adjective, as in *the door fell off its hinges*) does not require an apostrophe.